Supreme de [...]

ut off the supremes [...]
[...]ey are wanted cu[...]
[...]ege, with the carcas[...]
[...]ouillon her make a[...]
[...]aur dish up the supreme, th[...]
ordure, and fill in the centre with a
[...]yout of cockscombs truffle cut
Sauce over

Cotelettes Reform

[...]hites of eggs tongue truffle cut in
[...]fulienne, and the trimming chopped up
[...]sed to coat the cutlets with eggs &
[...]read [...]
[...]ule
[...]nd
[...]nd

Caneton a la Presse
Roast the duckling strangled [...]
[...] minutes on each side, and 2 on the
[...] in and cut into wee
[...]eeny &[...] [...] and put on a dish
[...]low milk suga[...] [...]es in a pan, with[...]
[...]hites beaten [...]ery, and one of bran[...]
[...]t in small pieces [...] duck in a press [...]
[...] are poured [...] last drop, of blood;
[...]s then covered [...]spoon of butter in a[...]
[...] after the souffle [...]les, add a glass of pe[...]
[...]eunte dust over [...]ndy, salt & cayenne
[...]unnle [...]tch fire, when the fir[...]
[...] [...] duck blood and
[...] of strawberry [...]eedily cook for 2 mi[...]
[...]eering a vanilla [...]u still boiling over the
[...]in the place of [...] and serve

CHURCHILL'S COOKBOOK

IMPERIAL WAR MUSEUMS

CHURCHILL'S COOKBOOK

Georgina Landemare

Foreword by Lady Churchill

Introduction by Phil Reed,
Former Director of Churchill War Rooms

Published by IWM, Lambeth Road, London SE1 6HZ
iwm.org.uk

© Edwina Brocklesby, 2019
Introduction © The Trustees of the Imperial War Museum, 2019

ISBN 978-1-904897-73-6

A catalogue record for this book is available from the British Library.
Printed and bound in Italy by Printer Trento.

MIX
Paper | Supporting
responsible forestry
FSC® C015829

With thanks to Eddie Brocklesby,
granddaughter of Georgina Landemare, for her support.
Thanks also to Phil Reed, Elizabeth Bowers, Madeleine James,
Caitlin Flynn, Abigail Lelliott, and the staff of IWM.

CONTENTS

A framed photograph of Clementine Churchill given as a gift
to Georgina Landemare.

I have all my life had a taste for cooking, having inherited this interest from my mother and grandmother.

I have known Mrs Landemare for a long time – in fact since the early twenties. Her husband, with whom she had worked for many years, was a renowned chef; and when he died she decided to do temporary work. She used to visit Scotland in the autumn, Newmarket during racing weeks, and in London she cooked the most delicious dinners and ball suppers.

Mrs Landemare used to come to Chartwell for weekend parties because in those days I had eager but inexperienced young cooks, and to them she would impart as much of her knowledge and skill as they were able to absorb. And so, when at the outbreak of war in 1939, Mrs Landemare came to see me and offered us her full-time services, I was enchanted because I knew she would be able to make the best out of rations and that everyone in the household would be happy and contented. She then remained with me for fifteen years, and when in 1954 she retired, I was at a loss.

Mrs Landemare's food is distinguished. She is an inspired intuitive cook, and it is I who encouraged her to write this book. I hope her readers will find it of value, but I expect they will have to try again and again before they get the magic touch.

Clementine S. Churchill

INTRODUCTION

On the night of 14 October 1940, a Luftwaffe bomb destroyed the old Treasury building in Whitehall. What Hitler had come close to achieving with that lucky strike was the elimination of Britain's wartime leader, Winston Churchill, who was in Number 10 Downing Street when the air raid took place. Churchill instructed his cook, Mrs Landemare, who had been reluctant to leave a pudding she was making, to join him in the rudimentary basement shelter. Blast from the explosion took out the back wall of the building, destroying the kitchen where they had both been just minutes before. The experience finally forced Churchill to use the marginally better protected Cabinet War Rooms as shelter in future. Churchill had, that night, one of the many brushes with death that he experienced throughout his long life. Just three minutes later, as he recounts in his memoirs, the very spot where they had both been standing became a scene of complete devastation.

The loss of his cook would most certainly have been a tragedy for Churchill, who was a legendary *bon vivant*. His frequently quoted quip, 'I am easily satisfied, I like the best', was borne out by his expensive tastes in champagne (Pol Roger), cognac (Hine), cigars (Romeo y Julieta), tailors (Turnbull and Asser), bootmakers (Lobb) and hatters (Lock & Co). Churchill dined at the best restaurants and was very particular about his food. At the outbreak of war in 1939, the already widely-feted cook, Georgina Landemare, renowned for her culinary skills at such high society occasions as the races at Newmarket, weekends at Cowes and debutante balls, offered her services to the Churchills for the duration of the war. It was, as Mrs Landemare later divulged in a BBC interview with Joan Bakewell, her 'war work'.

Georgina Landemare had known the Churchill family since the 1930s, when Churchill's wife Clementine occasionally employed her to cook for house parties at Chartwell. At these she had impressed Churchill, the demanding trencherman, and his eminent guests, with her often deceptively simple but exacting recipes. Clementine later recalled that when Mrs Landemare made her offer to cook for the Churchills, she was 'enchanted, because I knew she would be able to make the best out of rations and that everyone in the household would be happy and contented'. An arrangement that should have lasted for just six years of war continued until 1954 when, at the age of 72, Georgina Landemare finally retired – a year before Winston Churchill himself resigned as prime minister.

The details of Georgina Landemare's life are sketchy, but we do know she was the daughter (one of five children) of a coachman and entered service at the age of 14, working as a scullery maid to a wealthy gentleman in Kensington Palace Gardens. In 1909, by now a kitchen maid working for a wealthy family at their home in Gloucester Square, Paddington, she married the distinguished French chef of the Ritz, Paul Landemare, 25 years her senior and a recently widowed father of five. We do not know how they came to meet, but Georgina and Paul remained together until his death in 1932. They lived in Holland Park and Pimlico, areas both decidedly less grand then than they are today. Georgina appears to have had no formal training as a chef, but to have acquired her culinary skills from Paul. His expertise in French cuisine undoubtedly influenced her own style of cooking, but it still retained a distinctive English flavour. This suited Winston Churchill's traditional yet sophisticated palate. Churchill's youngest daughter Lady Soames later described Georgina's style as 'fashionable English country house cooking, but with a French touch, simply, but beautifully presented'.

That Winston Churchill was fond of his food has never been in doubt. 'It is well to remember', he said, 'that the stomach governs the world'. Mrs Landemare claimed, in that 1973 BBC interview with Joan Bakewell, that Winston Churchill 'was not a big eater', but it would be fair to say that the evidence indicates quite the opposite. At one small luncheon hosted by Churchill for King George VI at 10 Downing Street on 6 March 1941 (which Georgina Landemare almost certainly prepared) the menu comprised of 'fish patty, tournedos with mushrooms on top and braised celery and chipped potatoes, peaches and cheese to follow'. While perhaps not an especially large or rich repast, when taken in the context of wartime austerity and severe rationing, it suddenly takes on the scale of a feast.

The Churchills were in the happy position of owning their Chartwell estate, which included a farm that furnished them with eggs, milk, cream, chicken, pork and most vegetables, ingredients that ordinary mortals could rarely find in war-torn Britain (and even then usually in only small amounts). Mrs Landemare's recipes, despite her being attentive to the exigencies of the times, reflect the availability of these ingredients and Churchill's table must have been one to which an invitation would be keenly welcomed. Although his sympathy for the sufferings of the common man were legendary and real, his understanding sometimes fell short, as on the famous occasion when he finally let his secretary go home at 3am, with his kind permission to forego writing up her notes that night, but to have them ready by next morning. Indeed, when shown a plate of the everyday rations permitted to the average adult, he mumbled that it was 'not a bad meal' and was shocked to learn that he was being shown the basic rations for a whole week!

During the Blitz, both Chartwell and Chequers, the prime minister's country residence, were thought vulnerable to German attack. Arrangements were put in place for Churchill to spend weekends at Ditchley, in Oxfordshire, near his birthplace Blenheim Palace. Ditchley was the country residence of the wealthy Anglo-American Member of Parliament, Ronald Tree. Tree obtained from the Ministry of Food extra rations to entertain Churchill and his guests, who included Harry Hopkins – President Roosevelt's right-hand man – as well as the Chiefs of Staff, Cabinet members and close friends such as Lady Diana Cooper. Un-rationed game such as pheasant and grouse, to which Churchill was extremely partial, often appeared on the menu, and their leftovers, washed down with white wine, provided him with breakfast in bed the next morning.

Churchill was a man of routine – his two baths a day were accommodated throughout the war and wherever he was – with a penchant for holding scheduled meals with eminent individuals on a Tuesday. While almost all good fare was welcomed by Churchill, he did have his favourite dishes. The founder of the Churchill Centre, Richard Langworth, summarised his partiality for 'English traditional ... dishes like fowl, and roast beef with Yorkshire pudding. He preferred clear, "limpid" soups to thick, creamy ones. He enjoyed shellfish more than fish and Stilton more than sweet desserts', adding that 'he could easily be persuaded to take both of the latter'. Churchill's personal nurse, Roy Howells, writing in his book *Simply Churchill*, gives an even longer, more luxuriant list of his likes – including Dover Sole, Maryland Chicken, lobster, dressed crab, jugged hare ... and tinned Mandarin oranges. Among the many things Churchill took against, Howells lists 'tripe, currant cake, marmalade, stews and hot pots, Chinese foods and boiled eggs'.

A plaque that remains on a wall inside 10 Downing Street records that Churchill played host to the King at meals on 14 occasions between 1940 and 1945. During two of the meals, an enemy air bombardment forced the King and his Prime Minister to retreat into the neighbouring shelter. For Churchill, meals were occasions to engage in discussion of current issues, strategic matters and, above all, politics. Churchill was famed for his disquisitions, being anything but a receptive conversationalist. His witty remark that '[my idea of a good dinner] is to discuss good food, and after this good food has been discussed, to discuss a good topic – with myself the chief conversationalist' had more than a grain of truth in it.

Georgina Landemare was certainly kept busy by her charge (charges: she fed all members of the family at various times) and would meet daily with Clementine Churchill to discuss menus. Georgina's granddaughter recalled her grandmother telling her that she 'never went to bed till after Mr Churchill's last whiskey, and she was always up ready to cook him breakfast every morning'. Churchill would often change his mind about where he wanted to eat, and this entailed Georgina having to move her cooking equipment, ingredients and even complete meals between 10 Downing Street, the Cabinet War Rooms and the upstairs Annexe (the suite of offices above the Cabinet War Rooms which Churchill had converted to living and working space at the end of 1940 and where he lived until his defeat in the July 1945 General Election).

Despite all the challenges, stresses and strains in working for him, Georgina remained an ardent and faithful supporter of Winston and a lifelong friend of the Churchill family. She was with him on the day he was cast out of office in 1945 and stayed with him after the war, through the ups and downs of his political fortunes. Georgina was eventually encouraged by Lady Churchill, always a staunch devotee of her cooking, and by her own daughter, to write down the recipes of the food she cooked for the Prime Minister. It was no easy task, as Georgina had never recorded the weights of her ingredients, nor, as she had never seen them written down, the French names of the recipes. The resultant book, *Recipes From No. 10*, was published in 1958 and was for a long time a best-seller, before going out of print and becoming a collector's item.

Georgina outlived Churchill by 13 years and attended his state funeral on 30 January 1965. She died at the age of 96 in 1978, a year after Clementine passed away. Napoleon, for whom Churchill retained a lifelong admiration, once famously claimed that 'an army marches on its stomach'. For Churchill good food and a cook to prepare it were quintessential to his leading Britain at war. In Georgina Landemare, he found someone who, by sustaining him for six long years of conflict, played her own vital part in helping him to defeat his arch foe and antithesis, the vegetarian and teetotaller Adolf Hitler. Georgina Landemare's importance to Churchill was nicely and neatly illustrated on VE Day, 8 May 1945, when after giving his rousing speech to the massed crowds in Whitehall, he made a point of turning to his faithful chef and thanking her 'most cordially', saying he could not have managed all the way through the war without her.

Phil Reed
Former Director of Churchill War Rooms
London

Georgina Landemare, 1950

Above: The kitchen at 10 Downing Street, 1927
Top right: Entertaining guests: Churchill speaks at an official luncheon, 1941
Bottom right: The dining room at Chartwell, circa 1945

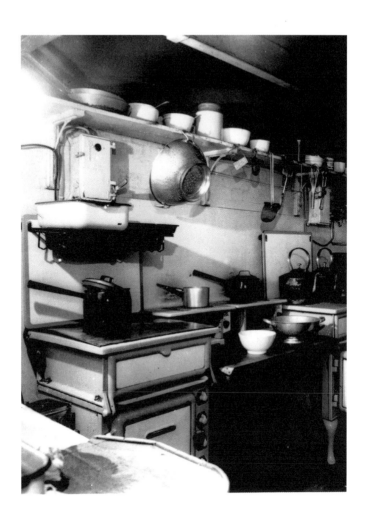

The Churchills' kitchen in the Cabinet War Rooms

CONVERSION CHARTS

DIMENSIONS

Imperial	Metric
1/8 inch	3 mm
¼ inch	5 mm
½ inch	1 cm
¾ inch	2 cm
1 inch	2.5 cm
1¼ inch	3 cm
1½ inch	4 cm
1¾ inch	4.5 cm
2 inch	5 cm
2½ inch	6 cm
3 inch	7.5 cm
3½ inch	9 cm
4 inch	10 cm
5 inch	13 cm
5¼ inch	13.5 cm
6 inch	15 cm
6½ inch	16 cm
7 inch	18 cm
7½ inch	19 cm
9 inch	20 cm
9½ inch	24 cm
10 inch	25.5 cm
11 inch	28 cm
12 inch	30 cm

WEIGHTS

Imperial	Metric
½ oz	10g
¾ oz	20g
1 oz	25g
1½ oz	40g
2 oz	50g
2½ oz	60g
3 oz	75g
3½ oz	90g
4 oz	110g
4½ oz	125g
5 oz	150g
6 oz	175g
7 oz	200g
8 oz (½ lb)	225g
9 oz	250g
10 oz	275g
12 oz (¾ lb)	350g
1 lb	450g
2 lb	900g
3 lb	1.35 kg

LIQUIDS

Imperial	Metric
1 teaspoon	5 ml
1 tablespoon	15 ml
4 tablespoons	55 ml
¼ pint	150 ml
½ pint	275 ml
¾ pint	450 ml
1 pint	570 ml
2 pints (1 quart)	1.2 litres
8 pints	4.8 litres
1 gill	150 ml

AMERICAN

American	Imperial	Metric
1 cup flour	5 oz	150g
1 cup caster/granulated sugar	8 oz	225g
1 cup brown sugar	6 oz	175g
1 cup butter/margarine/lard	8 oz	225g
1 cup sultanas/raisins	7 oz	200g
1 cup currants	5 oz	150g
1 cup ground almonds	4 oz	110g
1 cup golden syrup	12 oz	350g
1 cup uncooked rice	7 oz	200g
1 cup grated cheese	4 oz	110g

SOUP

POTAGE ALÉXANDRE

For six people.

1 pint flageolets and french beans mixed; good handful of sorrel; 2 pints stock; 2 egg yolks; ½ gill cream; seasoning.

Boil the flageolets and french beans for an hour in a pint of salted water. In another saucepan, melt the butter and add the sorrel, stirring well until softened. Pass the cooked beans through a sieve into the saucepan containing the sorrel, and add the 2 pints of stock. Bring all to the boil.

Beat the yolks of eggs and the cream in the soup tureen and then pour in the soup, gently mixing with a wooden spoon.

POTAGE ARGENTEUIL

This soup should be made from the water in which Argenteuil asparagus has been cooked as a vegetable. Tinned asparagus is almost as good and if this is used the liquor can be diluted.

For six people.

1 quart Argenteuil asparagus water; 1 cup rice; handful sorrel leaves ; 1 egg yolk; seasoning.

Melt a little butter in a saucepan with the sorrel and stir to prevent it catching. When soft, add the quart of asparagus water and the cupful of well-washed rice with seasoning. Cook for 20 minutes.

Beat the yolk of an egg in the soup tureen, add a little butter and then pour in the contents of the saucepan, stirring gently.

BORTSCH POLONAISE

For six people.

Duck carcass; celery root; parsley stalks; small branch fennel; little marjoram; peppercorns; 3 scraped raw beetroot; 3 carrots; 2 leeks; 1 cooked beetroot; cubes of duck meat and beef; sour cream; beetroot juice.

Make a consommé of the carcass, together with 1 quart of water, parsley stalks, chopped celery, fennel, a pinch of marjoram, 8 peppercorns, scraped raw beetroot, carrots, leeks and seasoning. Cook slowly for 1 hour. Strain and remove fat. Garnish with Julienne of cooked leeks, cooked beetroot, small cubes of beef and duck. Serve separately sour cream and juice extracted from the cooked beetroot.

CONSOMMÉ

Producing approximately 4 quarts.

6 lb leg of beef; 4 lb knuckle of veal; 5 carrots; 6 onions; 3 leeks; 2 turnips; peppercorns; 4 cloves; bouquet garni; blade of mace; green of a head of celery.

Cut up the meat in large pieces and put into a stockpot with salt and 2 gallons of water. Break up the bones and brown in a sharp oven. When sufficiently done add them to the above liquid and bring to the boil slowly. Chop all the vegetables roughly and fry well and add to the stock, together with peppercorns, cloves, mace and seasoning. Simmer very gently for 6 hours. Skim well; strain through a fine cloth. Remove fat and keep consommé till required.

The bones, etc. remaining after the consommé has been strained can be left as a basis for a second stock.

CREAM OF BROAD BEANS

For four people.

1 pint shelled broad beans; 2 onions; 4 parsley sprigs; 4 sage leaves; 1½ pints milk; 1 oz butter; cream and seasoning.

Fry onions in butter, add the beans, parsley, sage and milk. Cook slowly for ¾ hour. Pass through a fine sieve. Replace the purée in a saucepan and bring to the boil. Add a little cream and sprinkle with chopped parsley before serving.

CRÈME DE CONCOMBRES GLACÉ

For four people.

1 cucumber; 6 spring onion tops; 2 medium potatoes; butter; 1 pint white stock; 1 gill cream; tarragon.

Cut up cucumber, the tops of spring onions, 2 medium peeled potatoes. Put into a saucepan a knob of butter. When melted, add the cucumber, onions and potatoes and stir well. When the butter has been absorbed, add 1 pint of white stock; season well and cook until quite soft. Pass through a sieve, put into a basin and add a gill of cream and shreds of tarragon. Keep in a refrigerator and serve in cups.

CRÈME DUBARRY

For four people.

1 cauliflower; butter; 1½ pints white stock; 2 egg yolks; a little cream; chervil.

Cook very slowly some branches of white cauliflower till tender, in butter and white stock. Season well and pass through a sieve. Put the purée back into a saucepan and bring to the boil.

Now add 2 yolks of eggs with a little cream, taking care that it does not boil once the egg yolks are added. Garnish with small cooked branches of cauliflower and sprigs of chervil.

CRÈME JEANETTE

For four people.

3 each of onions, carrots, parsnips, leeks, turnips; ¼ green part of a cabbage; 1 pint milk and water mixed; good knob of butter; 2 tablespoons fine sago; watercress and chervil.

Cut all the vegetables into rounds with a small sized cutter, and fry lightly in a little butter. Add the milk mixture and seasoning and cook for 20 minutes. Sprinkle in the sago and allow to cook for a further 10 minutes. Garnish with sprigs of watercress and chervil, adding a little butter and cream when serving.

CRÈME NORVÉGIENNE

For six people.

3 medium-sized onions; 2 large swedes; Julienne of cooked beetroot; 1 egg yolk; cream and seasoning; 1½ pints water or stock.

Cut the onions and fry in butter and when cooked add the swedes chopped finely. To this add either 1½ pints of water or stock. Bring to the boil and allow to cook slowly for an hour. Pass the whole through a fine sieve and if it is too thick add a little more stock. This should then be poured slowly over the beaten egg yolks and cream, and Julienne beetroot.

CRÈME VICHYSOISE

For four people.

White part of 1 dozen leeks; 1½ oz butter; 1 celery stick; 2 oz potato; 1 pint chicken consommé; a small bunch of parsley tied with string; salt, pepper and nutmeg; 3 tablespoons cream.

Melt the butter in a saucepan over a slow heat; put in the leeks, cut up into small slices. Cook slowly for 15 minutes until a golden colour, stirring slowly and carefully. Add sliced potatoes cut thinly, also celery and parsley, salt, pepper and nutmeg to taste; then the chicken consommé. Bring to the boil, stir well and simmer for ½ hour until vegetables are well cooked. Remove parsley. If desired, the soup can be passed through a sieve, but it is not necessary.

Leave to get cold, then add the cream. Keep well iced before serving, and at the last sprinkle a little chopped parsley.

HOCHEPOT À LA FLAMANDE

For six people.

Pig's tail, ears and feet; ½ lb salted pork; ½ lb lean beef; ½ lb lean mutton; carrots; onions; cabbage; potatoes; minced leeks; water.

Place in a saucepan the pig's tail, ears, feet, salted pork, lean beef and mutton; cover with water. Add carrots, onions, cabbage, potatoes and minced leeks. Cook for 1 hour, or longer, until the meat is tender.

Remove the meat and vegetables from the soup and serve as a separate dish.

PETITE MARMITE

This should be made with the consommé as given in the basic recipe.

Tie together carrots, leeks, cabbage, celery and onions. Brown an old hen in the oven. Place the vegetables and old hen in the saucepan with the amount of consommé required and cook slowly for 3 hours. When serving, the vegetables may be cut up with the hen and served in the soup. Special marmite pots should be used for this soup which should be accompanied by thin toast.

May be served with grated Parmesan cheese.

FRENCH POT-AU-FEU SOUP

For ten people.

3 lb shoulder of beef; 2 quarts cold water; 3 carrots, turnips, leeks; ½ cabbage; salt to taste; 6 peppercorns.

Put on a stewpan with cold water and beef, bring to the boil. Skim well; this operation should take about 10 minutes. The soup must no longer boil quickly, but just simmer gently. Add vegetables whole, first tying up cabbage, and simmer for about 5 hours. If the cooked giblets of a fowl are available and added, ½ hour before serving, it will give a more delicate flavour.

It is now time to remove the fat. A quantity of the soup is ladled out into a saucepan, allowed to boil and thickened with tapioca, or simply poured into the soup tureen over rounds of fried bread. Add vegetables, in large dice, and meat.

POTAGE BONNE FEMME

For six people.

4 leeks; 4 nice-sized potatoes; 1 oz butter; 4 lettuce leaves; 1½ pints chicken broth; 2 egg yolks; a little cream; seasoning.

Mince the leeks and potatoes very fine and fry lightly without browning. Stirring well, add broth and seasoning. Cook for 35 minutes slowly.

Blanch the lettuce leaves in salted water, shred and mix with the soup and at the last minute add the liaison of egg yolks and cream.

Pieces of french roll, cut thinly and browned in the oven, or else fried croutons, can be served with the soup.

POTAGE CRÉCY

For four people.

1 pint veal stock; 8 carrots; ¼ lb rice; 2 onions; seasoning; 1 gill thin cream.

Chop the onion and fry lightly in a saucepan. Add the outer part of the carrots, rice, seasoning and veal stock. Cook altogether slowly for 1 hour. Pass through a fine sieve and add a little cream.

Note
Turnip, celery and artichoke soup can be made in the same manner, but omitting the rice.

POTAGE MILANAISE

For four people.

1 lb tomatoes; 2 oz rice; 1 small onion; sprig of thyme, 1 quart water; 1 oz butter; seasoning; stock; cream.

Place in a saucepan an ounce of butter; when it is melted, add tomatoes, a handful of well-washed rice, a small onion cut finely and a small sprig of thyme. Stir well with a wooden spoon, adding salt and pepper. Now add a quart of water and cook slowly until the rice is quite cooked. Pass all through a sieve and add some stock if the purée is too thick. A little butter with cream should be put into the tureen, and the soup poured on to it.

POTAGE PARMENTIER

For six people.

White portion of 3 leeks; 3 or 4 potatoes; a little chervil; butter; 1 cup boiled milk; 1 quart water; cream; few cubes of fried bread; seasoning.

This is a very simple soup but should be prepared carefully; it is quickly made and is not expensive.

Melt an ounce of butter in a saucepan, slice the leeks very finely; add to the butter and allow to cook, uncovered, very slowly for about 10 minutes. Then add about a quart of water, salt to taste and the potatoes which should be cut up. In about 20 minutes leeks and potatoes will be cooked. The water should be separated and the remainder passed through a hair sieve. Now add purée to the strained water and bring to the boil, stirring all the time.

A handful of cubes of bread are browned in a frying pan with a little butter, and should be placed in the tureen, together with hot milk and cream, a lump of butter about the size of a large egg, a pinch of chopped chervil leaves. Pour in soup over the bread, etc.

VELOUTÉ DE POISSON JEAN BART

For four people.

1 pint very good fish stock; small quenelles of fish; 2 tomatoes; 3 tablespoons small cooked macaroni; Julienne of cooked leeks; cream; paprika.

Bring to the boil the pint of fish stock, add the diced, skinned and seeded tomatoes, macaroni, Julienne of leeks, cream and a pinch of paprika. Lastly, garnish with quenelles of fish.

VELOUTÉ HOMARD À LA CLEVELAND

For four people.

1 cooked lobster; 1 chopped onion; 1½ pints fish stock or water; 2 cooked potatoes; butter; seasoning; cream; 2 egg yolks; brandy.

Remove the flesh of the lobster from the shell. Chop finely the shell, together with the onion and place in a saucepan with 1½ pints of water, or fish stock if available. Cook for 1 hour, strain and add to it the flesh of the lobster which should be cut into dice. Bring to the boil once again, adding the dice of cooked potatoes, butter and seasoning.

Place in the tureen, cream and 2 egg yolks blended together. Now add the soup and at the last moment a teaspoonful of brandy.

FISH

FISH ASPIC

2 quarts fish stock; 2 carrots; 2 leeks; 3 oz gelatine; 3 egg whites and shells; 3 tablespoons tarragon vinegar; 2 tablespoons chilli vinegar; few parsley stalks; 6 crushed peppercorns; salt.

Put the fish stock into a saucepan with the finely chopped vegetables, parsley stalks, crushed peppercorns, vinegars, gelatine and salt. Leave to stand for 10 minutes or until the gelatine is dissolved. Add the whites and crushed shells of the eggs, whisk well and bring slowly to the boil. Simmer for 10 minutes. Remove from heat and allow to stand for a few minutes before straining through a fine cloth. Leave to set.

FISH STOCK

Bones of whiting or any white fish; leeks; carrots; onions; bouquet garni; seasoning.

Chop up the fish bones, put into a saucepan with the roughly cut vegetables, bouquet garni and seasoning. Boil slowly for 1 hour, strain up and use as required.

COQUILLES ST. JACQUES ITALIENNE

For eight people.

6 scallops; ½ lb mushrooms; Béchamel sauce; shallot; butter; seasoning

Blanch and chop up 6 scallops. Allow to cool. Make a Béchamel sauce with fish stock, add the chopped scallops and some chopped cooked mushrooms, which have been cooked with a little shallot, salt and pepper. Place the mixture in a fireproof dish with little pieces of butter and bake for about 10 minutes.

CRAB OMAHA

½ lb cold cooked crab meat; 2 hard-boiled eggs; ½ cucumber; 4 tomatoes; 2 tablespoons mayonnaise; a little tabasco; ½ teaspoon mixed mustard; 1 tablespoon each tarragon and chilli vinegar; 1 tablespoon cream; salt and pepper.

Chop up cooked crab meat, hard-boiled eggs, cucumber which has been seeded but not skinned, and tomatoes skinned and seeded.

Place in a bowl the 2 tablespoons mayonnaise, tabasco, mixed mustard, tarragon and chilli vinegar, cream, salt and pepper. Mix well, add the crab meat, etc. and put into a glass bowl previously lined with crisp lettuce leaves. Serve with brown bread and butter sandwiches.

CROUSTADES OF LOBSTER

For six people.

1 cooked medium lobster; ½ pint fish stock; slices of bread, 1 inch thick; ¼ lb mushrooms; few shrimps; seasoning.

Remove shell from lobster, crush and cook in fish stock for ½ hour. Strain.

Cut out as many croustades as required with a 2-inch plain cutter, scoop out the centres and fry in deep fat.

Cut into small dice the flesh of a lobster and some cooked mushrooms. Add a few shrimps. Make velouté sauce with the stock from the shells, add the lobster flesh, mushrooms, etc. and fill the croustades which should be very hot.

ÉPERLANS À LA MÉTÉOR

For six people.

6 large smelts; ½ lb mushrooms; 2 oz breadcrumbs; 2 shallots; 6 anchovy fillets; chopped parsley; lemon juice; egg yolk; anchovy sauce; seasoning.

Clean some smelts, remove the bone. Mix together chopped cooked mushroom, lemon juice, parsley, breadcrumbs, chopped shallot, oil and seasoning. Place a little of this stuffing on each smelt, cover with an anchovy fillet and roll them up, fastening with a skewer. Flour, egg and breadcrumb and fry in deep fat. When cooked, remove skewer and serve with fried parsley and anchovy sauce.

KOULEBIAKA

For six people.

2 lb fresh salmon; ½ lb cooked rice; ½ lb chopped raw mushrooms; 3 hard-boiled eggs; parsley; 2 shallots; butter; seasoning; ¾ lb puff pastry.

Cook salmon in salted water and stand aside until cold. Remove the fish from the stock, flake, and add to it ½ lb of dry cooked rice, chopped raw mushrooms, 3 finely chopped hard-boiled eggs, and parsley, chopped shallots, salt and pepper. Mix well, adding a little oiled butter.

Roll out the puff pastry, put in the mixture, fold over, moisten and seal the edges. Make a small slit on the top of the pastry. Brush over with melted butter and cook for ¾ hour in a moderate oven.

Serve with hot horseradish sauce.

ROUGETS FRANCILLON

For four people.

4 red mullet; croutons of fried bread; anchovy butter; sauce Provençale.

Clean some small red mullet, make an incision on either side of the fish and grill. Fry some croutons and smear with anchovy butter. Place each fish on a crouton and pour over some sauce Provençale.

Serve with straw potatoes.

FILLETS OF SOLE DUGLÉRÉ

Fillets of sole as required; 2 shallots; fish stock; 3 tomatoes; parsley stalks; seasoning; butter.

Skin the fillets, lay them in a buttered fireproof dish with chopped shallots, tomatoes skinned, seeded and cut up in pieces, and parsley stalks. Cover with good fish stock and seasoning and poach in the oven until cooked. Strain off stock and remove parsley stalks. Make a sauce with this stock, adding the tomato and plenty of butter.

Cover the fish with this sauce and replace in oven to brown.

FILLETS OF SOLE ÉLAINE

For four people.

4 fillets of sole; 4 oz grated Parmesan cheese; 3 oz oiled butter; 3 tablespoons Béchamel sauce; ¼ lb mushrooms; seasoning.

First fry 4 fillets of sole lightly in butter and keep hot. Thinly slice the mushrooms and cook in butter.

Mix well together the Béchamel sauce, grated cheese, oiled butter and a pinch of cayenne pepper. Keep hot.

Place the cooked fillets in a greased fireproof dish, then a layer of the mushrooms. Pour over the sauce and put under the grill to brown.

FILLETS OF SOLE MARGUERY

For four people.

4 fillets of sole; 2 egg yolks; fleurons of puff pastry for garnish; 6 oysters; shrimps; seasoning.

Poach 4 fillets of sole in the stock made from the bones. Remove the fillets and reduce the liquor to about half the quantity, add 2 yolks of eggs and a little cream. Coat the fillets with this sauce and garnish with oysters, shrimps which have been heated in melted butter, and fleurons of puff pastry.

FILLETS OF SOLE ORLY

For four people.

4 fillets of sole; 1 sliced onion; 1 sliced carrot; parsley stalks; seasoning; oil; ¼ lb flour; water; egg white; tomato sauce; parsley.

Cut the fillets in halves, place in a dish with onion, carrot, parsley stalks and seasoning. Cover with oil and leave from 4 to 6 hours, turning them occasionally.

Make a batter with the flour and water, adding the egg white, which must be stiffly whipped. Remove the fillets from the marinade, dip in the batter and fry quickly in deep boiling fat.

Serve with tomato sauce and garnish with fried parsley.

QUENELLES OF FISH

2 whiting; 2 tablespoons stiff cold Béchamel sauce; fish stock; 2 egg whites; 1 gill cream; seasoning.

Skin the fish and remove flesh from the bones. Pass through a fine mincer. Mix with the Béchamel sauce and egg whites, season and pound all together and pass through a very fine wire sieve. Place the mixture in a basin and stand in crushed ice. Gradually stir in the gill of cream.

Shape the mixture like small eggs, using 2 teaspoons and passing mixture from one to the other. This size is for soup only; if quenelles are desired for any other purpose, table or dessert spoons should be used.

Place the quenelles on a buttered pan, cover with a little fish stock and poach carefully till firm.

SOLES CHAMPEAUX

Fillets of sole; white wine; fish stock; butter; a little cream; a few blanched shrimps; Julienne of carrots; seasoning.

Poach as many fillets as required in seasoned white wine and fish stock. When cooked remove fillets and make a sauce with the liquor. Add a little fresh butter, cream, a few blanched shrimps and Julienne of cooked carrots. Pour over the soles and serve very hot.

SOLE MÂCONAISE

For six people.

6 fillets of sole; 3 tablespoons each red wine and fish stock; blade of garlic; bouquet of herbs; ¼ lb mushrooms; 18 button onions; butter; cream; seasoning.

Place fillets of sole in a greased fireproof dish, cover with red wine and fish stock, a blade of garlic, a bouquet of herbs, mushrooms cut into 4 pieces, and cover with greased paper. Cook slowly.

Cook separately 18 small button onions in butter till tender and without browning.

Remove the fish from the fireproof dish, also the bouquet garni. Place ready for serving and arrange mushrooms and button onions around fillets. Make a sauce with the liquor left from the fillets, adding a little fresh butter and cream. Pour over the fish.

SOUFFLÉ OF SOLE

For six people.

6 fillets of sole; 3 whiting; a little live lobster spawn; 2 egg yolks and whites; Hollandaise sauce; 6 oysters.

Fold and place fillets of sole in a greased fireproof dish.

Take the flesh of 3 whiting and a little lobster spawn. Pound together, season well and pass through a fine sieve. Add egg yolks and the whites whipped stiffly. Put all on top of the fillets and cook in a medium oven for 15 minutes.

Serve with Hollandaise sauce to which oysters have been added.

TROUT REINE MARIE

1½ lb trout; 3 egg yolks; ¼ pint salmon stock; 4 oz butter; 1 tablespoon tomato purée; cream; bouquet garni; aubergine; 6 small tomatoes; sprig of mint; 12 button mushrooms; small new potatoes.

Sauté the trout with herbs in reduced fish stock for 45 minutes in a slow oven. When cooked remove skin and place on dish for serving.

Make a sauce by beating together egg yolks with a ¼ pint of salmon stock, butter, tablespoon tomato purée, little cream. Place the bowl on a saucepan of boiling water, season well, and whisk until it is thick and creamy. Thinly coat the fish with a little of this sauce and serve the remainder separately.

Garnish
Cut the aubergine in slanting slices and sauté in hot butter. Skin and seed the tomatoes and sauté in hot butter with a little chopped mint and a few small mushrooms and seasoning. Serve small potatoes separately.

TROUT ROYALE

1½ lb trout; 2 pints Court Bouillon; small potatoes; cucumber.

Court Bouillon
Boil together 4 pints water, salt, few peppercorns, 5 tablespoons vinegar, 1 carrot, 1 onion and a bouquet garni.

Cook the trout in Court Bouillon for 20 minutes, remove skin and serve with a Bercy sauce. Garnish with small new potatoes and blanched cucumber cut in large sections.

FILLETS OF TURBOT BÉARNAISE

For four people.

2 lb turbot; egg and breadcrumbs; small potatoes; Béarnaise sauce.

Fillet the turbot and remove the skin. Wash, dry, salt and flour each fillet, dip into beaten egg and cover with breadcrumbs.

Melt a small amount of butter in a frying pan and when it steams add the fillets and brown slowly on both sides.

Serve on a long dish with groups of freshly boiled small new potatoes and a border of Béarnaise sauce.

Serve separately Béarnaise sauce.

FILLETS OF WHITING FARCIS

For eight people.

4 whiting; 4 oz chopped shrimps; 3 tablespoons fine white breadcrumbs; 1 teaspoon anchovy essence; 2 tablespoons white sauce; 2 egg yolks; a little butter; fish stock; seasoning.

Fillet and skin the whiting. Flatten the fillets with a heavy palette knife.

Stuffing
Mix together chopped shrimps, breadcrumbs, anchovy essence, white sauce, egg yolks and oiled butter. Spread over each fillet, roll up and poach in good fish stock made from the bones.

Make a velouté sauce with the liquor and serve very hot.

WHITING CECILIA

Fillets of whiting as required, 1 egg yolk, butter, asparagus points, potatoes, seasoning, grated Parmesan cheese.

Fillet and skin whiting as needed, season well, dip in yolk of egg and fry in oiled butter. Serve with asparagus tips and olive shaped potatoes. Sprinkle with grated cheese and put under the grill at the last moment.

WHITING DORIA

For six people.

3 whiting; lemon juice; ¼ lb butter; chopped parsley; potatoes; cucumber.

Fillet and skin the whiting, flour well, and fry lightly in half the amount of butter. Melt and brown the remainder of the butter, add lemon juice and chopped parsley and seasoning. Pour this mixture over the fish and serve very hot.

Garnish with potatoes and cucumber cooked and cut into small olive-shaped pieces.

FRIED CUTLETS OF SALMON

For four people.

1 lb salmon; 3 oz breadcrumbs; milk; 1 egg yolk; a little cream; parsley; seasoning.

Put salmon through a mincing machine, mix with breadcrumbs soaked in milk, season well and add 1 yolk of egg and a little cream. Mix into a paste and shape into a cutlet. Egg and breadcrumb and fry in deep fat.

Serve with fried crisp parsley.

DARNE DE SAUMON VERNET

For six people.

2 lb middle cut of salmon; 1 gill fish stock; 1 teaspoon anchovy essence; 2 oz butter; 1 oz flour; 1 truffle; 6 mushrooms; 1 hard-boiled egg white; 2 gherkins; small cooked potatoes.

Grease a fireproof dish and lay in some ½-inch thick slices of salmon cut from the skinned thick part of the fish. Pour over the fish stock, season, cover with greased paper and poach in the oven for 10 minutes.

Make a sauce in the ordinary way with butter, flour, fish stock, anchovy essence, Julienne strips of truffle, mushrooms, white of hard-boiled eggs and gherkins. Mask over the pieces of cooked salmon with the sauce and serve with small cooked potatoes.

SOUFFLÉ DE MERLUCHE FUMÉE

For four people.

1 medium-sized dried haddock; milk; 3 egg yolks; 2 oz oiled butter; cream; seasoning; ¼ lb short pastry; potatoes.

Line a medium-sized flan ring with short pastry and cook without colouring. Remove ring, grease a strip of paper about 4 inches wide to go round the outside of the pastry case as for a soufflé.

Cook a dried haddock in milk, remove all flesh from the bones and chop very finely. Season well, add a little cream, oiled butter, yolks of eggs and the whites stiffly whipped. Place all in the flan case and bake for 15 minutes. Remove paper and serve with small boiled potatoes.

EGGS

COLD EGGS TZIGANE

For six people.

6 eggs; 6 oz spaghetti; 3 gills cream; 2 tablespoons Worcester sauce; 1 teaspoon mixed mustard; 1 tablespoon tomato ketchup; 6 tomatoes.

Cook the spaghetti in salted water and when cooked dry on a cloth and cut into inch lengths. Put into a bowl 3 gills of cream and whip up until it is stiff. Add salt, pepper, teaspoonful of mixed mustard, Worcester sauce, tomato ketchup, and the cooked spaghetti. Mix well and place in a glass dish.

Hard boil 6 eggs and when cold cut into quarters lengthwise. Arrange alternately with quarters of tomatoes which have been skinned and seeded. This must be served very cold.

CREAM EGGS

Eggs as required; Mornay sauce; cream; seasoning; tomato sauce.

Make a stiff Mornay sauce and add 2 egg yolks. Grease dariole moulds with clarified butter, and coat with the sauce. Break an egg into each mould and season. Whip some fresh cream and fill the moulds to the top. Bake in a very moderate oven until set. Turn out and serve with a good tomato sauce.

CUTLETS OF EGGS

For six people.

4 hard-boiled eggs; 1 egg yolk; 4 oz cooked tongue; 1 gill Béchamel sauce; 1 large shallot; knob of butter; seasoning; breadcrumbs; parsley.

Chop shallot finely and fry in butter without colouring.

Make 1 gill Béchamel sauce, add to it seasoning, shallot, hard-boiled eggs and tongue which should be finely chopped together. Mix lightly adding the yolk of egg. Place on a flat dish and allow to get cold.

Divide into portions and shape in cutlets. Flour, dip in egg and breadcrumbs, and fry in deep fat.

Serve with crisp fried parsley.

EGGS IN TOMATOES

Eggs and tomatoes as required; butter; a little cream; seasoning.

Skin and seed as many large tomatoes as required, season well. Grease a fireproof dish and place tomatoes. In each one break an egg and a small knob of butter. Pour over a little cream and cook in a medium oven.

MADRAS EGGS

For four people.

4 hard-boiled eggs; 6 skinned and seeded tomatoes; 4 oz chopped cooked ham; 2 shallots; 6 tablespoons curry sauce; 4 oz cooked rice.

Butter a fireproof dish well and into this place first a layer of sliced tomato, then of sliced eggs sprinkled with chopped shallot, pepper and salt, next a layer of curry sauce and of chopped ham. Repeat these layers and cover the top with boiled rice and knobs of butter. Bake in a moderate oven for ½ to ¾ hour.

OEUFS BÉNÉDICTINE

For six people.

6 eggs; 3 muffins; 6 slices of tongue; Hollandaise sauce.

Poach the 6 eggs and keep warm.

Cut muffins in half and toast. Butter well. Lay on each muffin a slice of tongue, place the poached egg on this, keeping all very hot. Before serving, cover with Hollandaise sauce.

OEUFS BERCEAU

For six people.

3 medium-sized potatoes; 6 eggs; 6 tablespoons minced cooked chicken; 3 tablespoons cream; seasoning.

Poach the 6 eggs.

Bake the potatoes in the skins. Cut in two lengthwise and take out the potato with a spoon. Line the inside of the skin with a little chopped chicken mixed with cream, pepper and salt. Put a poached egg in each and coat with sauce Aurore.

OEUFS CÉCILE

For six people.

6 poached eggs; 6 medium-sized potatoes; about 1 gill Mornay sauce; 1 egg yolk; butter; 1 oz grated Parmesan cheese; seasoning.

Bake the potatoes in their skins until soft. Cut off the tops and take out the potato with a teaspoon, taking care not to break the skin.

Pass the potato through a sieve, mix with yolk of egg, pepper, salt and butter.

Make about 1 gill of Mornay sauce and in each potato case put first a little of the sauce, then a poached egg and spoon over more sauce on top of the egg. Force the potato mixture around the edge with a forcing bag and rose pipe. Sprinkle the top with grated cheese and put in a hot oven to brown.

OEUFS ESCARLATES

For six people.

3 hard-boiled eggs; 4 egg yolks; 4 oz chopped tongue; butter; 5 tablespoons cream; 6 fried croutes.

Chop finely the 3 hard-boiled eggs and tongue, add cream and seasoning. Beat yolks of eggs and mix all together. Grease 6 small dariole moulds with clarified butter, put in mixture and steam very slowly. When quite set turn out on to fried croutes.

OEUFS FARCIS

For four people.

4 eggs; a little butter, salt, pepper, chopped parsley and chives; 1 gill cream; brown breadcrumbs.

Hard boil the 4 eggs. Remove shells and cut in half lengthwise. Take out the yolks and beat them together with the same amount of butter. Add salt, pepper, chopped parsley and chives. Fill the white halves with this mixture.

Butter a dish, add a little cream and place the eggs in the dish. Pour over a little cream, sprinkle with brown breadcrumbs and small amount of butter. Bake in a moderate oven for 20 minutes.

OEUFS FORESTIÈRE

Eggs as required; Julienne of bacon; purée of cooked mushroom; chopped parsley; seasoning.

Garnish the bottom of cocotte pots with a purée of mushroom. Break in an egg, add a little cream, seasoning and cook slowly until set. Before serving, add a little Julienne of bacon and chopped parsley that have been fried lightly.

OEUFS NIÇOISE

Eggs as required; mayonnaise sauce; ½ lb french beans; 1 lb tomatoes; little cooked potato.

Poach as many eggs as needed allowing one per person. When cold and dry, coat them with a stiff mayonnaise sauce.

Make a salad with cooked french beans, tomatoes skinned and seeded and cooked potatoes all cut into dice. Mix with a little mayonnaise, season well. Put the salad in a glass dish, place the eggs on the salad and serve very cold.

OEUFS PASTOURELLE

Eggs as required; ¼ lb mushrooms; Julienne of fried bacon; shallot; 3 lambs' kidneys, or as many as needed; chopped parsley; seasoning.

Put some oil in a pan, heat and break in eggs, singly. As the egg begins to set, take a palette knife and turn over the white one side to cover the yolk. Remove from pan and place eggs in a circle in a large dish or in individual dishes. Garnish with Julienne mushrooms sautéd with shallots and chopped parsley, and Julienne of fried bacon. On each egg place a half kidney which has been sautéd.

OEUFS À LA REINE

Eggs as required; minced cooked chicken; little cream; seasoning.

Mince a little chicken and blend with cream. Put a little into each cocotte pot and break in an egg. Season well and cook slowly until the egg is set. Before serving, spoon a very small amount of glaze around the edge of the egg.

OEUFS VALENTINE

Eggs as required; dice of cooked tomatoes and mushroom; cream; butter; a little good veal gravy; chopped truffle.

In each cocotte pot place a little diced tomato and mushroom blended with cream, butter and reduced veal gravy. Break an egg into each pot and cook slowly. Just before serving sprinkle a little chopped truffle over each egg.

OEUFS VICTORIA

For six people.

1 cooked medium lobster; 6 poached eggs; 1 oz Parmesan cheese; cream; butter; ½ teaspoon paprika, salt.

Cut up finely the flesh of a lobster and mix with a little cream and seasoning. Put in a fireproof dish and cook very slowly for a few minutes. Poach 6 eggs and lay on the top of the lobster. Make a good creamy sauce to which add a little grated cheese and paprika. Pour over the eggs and slightly brown under the grill. This must be served very hot.

OEUFS SUR LE PLAT AMÉRICAINE

Eggs as required; slices of cooked ham; seasoning.

Butter the dish in which the eggs are to be served.

Place in the dish slices of ham, allowing one for each portion. Break on to each slice an egg and cook in a moderate oven until set. Surround with a thread of tomato sauce before serving.

OEUFS SUR LE PLAT JOCKEY CLUB

For six people.

6 eggs; 6 chicken livers; ¼ lb veal kidney; 6 oz mushrooms; 6 rounds of fried bread; seasoning.

Cut and fry rounds of bread and coat each with a purée of cooked chicken livers. Place these in a dish ready for serving and keep hot. Melt some butter and cook 6 eggs in an omelette pan until the whites are set. Trim with a round cutter, placing one on each croute.

Slice and sauté the veal kidney. Garnish the centre of the dish with this sauté and Julienne of cooked mushrooms.

OEUFS SUR LE PLAT LORRAINE

For six people.

6 eggs; 6 rashers of bacon; 3 oz Gruyère cheese; little cream; seasoning.

Garnish a greased fireproof dish with the rashers of grilled bacon. Grate over this the 3 oz Gruyère cheese and on top break in 6 eggs. Coat with thick cream and cook in moderate oven until set.

OMELETTE AUX POMMES DE TERRE

For four people.

4 eggs; ½ lb diced cooked potato; butter; seasoning.

Break the eggs into a basin and beat lightly with a fork, add salt and pepper.

Melt a large lump of butter in an omelette pan, toss in the dice of cooked potato and fry lightly. Pour in the eggs, stir very slightly with a fork or whisk, and when set double over.

SOUFFLÉ OF EGGS AURORE

For four people.

7 eggs; 2 tablespoons tomato purée; 3 oz cheese; seasoning.

Poach 4 eggs and allow to get cold. Put round the outside of a soufflé dish folds of buttered paper.

Make a Mornay sauce, adding 3 egg yolks, 2 tablespoons of tomato purée, salt and pepper. Put a thin layer of the sauce at the bottom of the soufflé dish and lay in the poached eggs. Whip the 3 whites very stiff and add to the remainder of the mixture. Cover the poached eggs and bake for 10 minutes in a sharp oven. The eggs should be still soft when the soufflé is cooked.

SOUFFLÉ OF EGGS GRATINÉS

For four people.

3 eggs; Parmesan cheese; cream; seasoning.

Place in a bowl a little cream, salt, pepper, 2 oz of grated Parmesan cheese, and 3 yolks of eggs. Beat well for 10 minutes. Whip the whites of the 3 eggs very stiffly and fold into the mixture. Put all into a buttered charlotte mould and steam very carefully for 20 minutes. Remove from the mould and turn out on to greased paper.

When quite cold cut into slices. Line a fireproof dish with Mornay sauce, place in the slices of the soufflé and cover with sauce. Bake for 20 minutes in a hot oven. This should be served immediately.

POULTRY

AIGUILLETTES DE CANETON

For four people.

2 young ducklings; 4 oz foie gras; ½ pint Chaudfroid sauce; ½ pint aspic jelly.

Roast or braise the duckling and set aside until cool, overnight if possible.

Remove the fillets from breast of ducklings and cut lengthwise into as many ¼-inch slices as possible. Spread over with a thin coating of foie gras and trim into nice shapes. Mask them over with a Chaudfroid sauce and afterwards with aspic jelly made from the bones.

Arrange on a dish with chopped aspic and serve a cold compote of oranges and Morello cherries as a salad.

COQ AU VIN

For six people.

1 plump chicken; piece of bacon about ½ lb; 12 small onions; 12 button mushrooms; 2 tablespoons brandy; ½ pint Burgundy; bouquet garni; butter; seasoning; slices of lemon and fleurons of pastry for garnishing.

Cut the chicken into 6 pieces and the bacon into thick cubes. Melt some butter in a saucepan and brown the bacon together with the onions. When a golden colour, add the chicken, bouquet garni, mushrooms and seasoning. Cover the pan and cook quickly till all is brown. Remove lid, take off the fat and pour over 2 tablespoons of brandy. Flame the brandy, add the Burgundy and cook for ¾ hour. Make a thickening by creaming some butter and flour together and add this to the chicken just before serving.

Take out chicken, place on a dish and pour over the sauce. Garnish with slices of lemon and fleurons of puff pastry.

PERDREAU FROID

Young partridges as required; vine leaves; rashers of fat bacon; Chaudfroid sauce; aspic jelly.

Rub salt over each partridge, wrap in vine leaves and fat bacon and finally roll and tie securely in greaseproof paper. Plunge into boiling water for 30 minutes. Remove, and, making sure the paper is still intact, plunge into a basin of iced water. Leave in the iced water for 20 minutes. Unwrap each one and dry off with muslin.

Place on a dish, either whole or cut in halves, and cover with Chaudfroid sauce. Serve on a bed of aspic.

POULARDE LAMBERTYE FROIDE

For eight people.

1 large chicken; 1 lb cooked ox tongue; 1 quart white stock; 1½ pints Chaudfroid sauce; ¾ pint cream; aspic jelly.

Poach a chicken in good seasoned white stock, and when cooked place the breast downwards and leave until it is quite cold.

Remove the supremes, slice them lengthwise and cover with a white Chaudfroid sauce. Leave the legs on the carcass and remove all the breastbone.

Mince and pass through a fine sieve the cooked ox tongue, mix with it sufficient cream to make it into a firm paste. Place this mixture in the carcass of the chicken and mould into the proper shape of the bird. Mask all with Chaudfroid sauce, decorate with truffle and place on a dish with the supremes on a bed of aspic jelly finely chopped.

Serve with Salade Russe.

POULET AU BLANC

For six people.

1 chicken; 3 egg yolks; juice of 2 lemons; 2 onions; 2 oz butter; 1 oz flour; 2 tablespoons fresh cream; bouquet garni; seasoning.

Cut up the chicken and poach in salted water with the chopped onion and bouquet garni for an hour or more if necessary. Take a small saucepan, melt the butter, add a good tablespoon of flour; mix well and add slowly some of the stock from the chicken. Cook this slowly for 10 minutes. In the meantime, place the yolks and the cream in a bowl with the juice of the lemons and beat them well. Add this to the sauce gradually, taking care that the mixture does not boil.

Place the chicken in a pyramid on a very hot dish and pour over the sauce, which should be thick enough to completely mask the chicken.

POULET À LA KING

For four people.

1 cold boiled chicken; 3 tablespoons flour; 2 oz butter; 1 cup cream; 1 cup broth; 1 teaspoon lemon juice; 6 small mushrooms; ¼ green seeded pepper; 1 seeded pimento; seasoning; 2 egg yolks.

Put the butter into a saucepan and mix in the flour, stir well and add cream, broth, lemon juice, mushrooms, green and pimento pepper previously diced, and seasoning. Cook all together for about 10 minutes to ¼ hour, then add the chicken which should be cut into large dice. Simmer again for 10 minutes. Lastly add the 2 yolks of eggs mixed with a little cream. Do not boil or the yolks will curdle.

POULET SAUTÉ MARENGO

For six people.

1 good-sized chicken; 1 lb tomatoes; 6 mushrooms; parsley stalks, and chopped parsley; 3 tablespoons oil; 6 eggs; 6 croutons; glass white wine; a little stock.

Cut up the chicken into joints and sauté in oil. Add the white wine, tomatoes roughly cut up, a blade of garlic, parsley stalks, mushrooms, seasoning and a little stock. Cook under cover slowly until tender. Take up the chicken and put into a clean saucepan. Strain off the liquor, pour back over the chicken and reduce. If the sauce is too thin, add a little butter beaten together with flour.

Serve with fried eggs, croutons and chopped parsley.

SOUFFLÉ DE VOLAILLE FROID

For six people.

1 boiling fowl; ½ pint cream; bare ½ oz gelatine; 4 oz finely chopped ham; aspic jelly; seasoning.

Cook a boiling chicken and leave it breast downwards until cold in the stock.

Remove all the white flesh and put through a mincer and afterwards through a fine sieve. Season well. Lightly whip ½ pint of cream and add to the chicken purée together with the gelatine diluted in a little of the chicken stock.

Place a band of oiled paper around the outside of a good sized soufflé dish. Put half of the chicken cream into the dish, then a layer of very finely chopped ham and then the remainder of the creamed mixture. Put in a cool place until ready for use.

Remove band, sprinkle a little chopped aspic jelly on the top and serve with a salad of cold peas.

VOLAILLE BOHÉMIENNE FROIDE

For six people.

1 chicken; 2 oz butter; lemon juice; ½ oz paprika; ½ pint cream; ½ pint chicken stock; some strips of red tinned pimento; cooked button mushrooms; 1 oz flour.

Cut up chicken and bring to the boil in salted water. Strain up and cool.

Melt some butter in a saucepan and sauté the chicken lightly. Add ½ pint of good chicken stock, seasoning and cook slowly for 1 hour. Remove chicken and allow to cool.

Make a good sauce with butter, flour and the juice from the chicken, add seasoning and paprika and simmer for 20 minutes. Cool off. Mix in ½ pint of cream and a squeeze of lemon juice.

Place the chicken on a glass dish, pour over the sauce and cut up strips of pimento, and add button mushrooms. Ice before serving.

VOLAILLE SULTANE FROIDE

For six people.

1 chicken; 1 onion; 1 oz curry powder; 1 oz flour; ½ pint Chablis; ½ pint water; 1 breakfast cup cream; 3 pimentoes; seasoning; oil and butter for frying.

Cut up a chicken into joints and fry lightly in oil and butter without colouring, add seasoning, curry powder and an onion chopped finely. Now add 1 oz of flour and stir gently until the flour is absorbed. Add the ½ pint of Chablis and ½ pint of water and cook slowly until done. Remove from heat and add 1 breakfast cup of cream and 3 pimentoes cut into dice. Cool off.

Serve very cold in a glass dish with a crisp lettuce salad.

MEAT

ASPIC JELLY

2 quarts meat stock; 2 carrots; 2 onions; 1 small stick of celery; 3 oz gelatine; 3 egg whites and shells; 4 tablespoons Madeira; bouquet garni; peppercorns; 2 cloves; seasoning.

Put the stock into a saucepan, first making quite sure it is free of fat. Add the finely chopped vegetables, bouquet garni, gelatine and seasoning. Allow to stand for 10 minutes or until the gelatine is dissolved. Add the whites and crushed shells of the eggs, whisk well and slowly bring to the boil, simmer for 10 minutes. Remove from heat and allow to stand a few minutes before straining through a fine cloth. Add the Madeira, and leave to set.

MEAT GLAZE

Leg of beef bones and knuckle of veal bones; carrots; turnips; onions cut up roughly; seasoning.

Chop the bones and brown in a sharp oven for 10 minutes. Remove and put all the bones in a large saucepan with plenty of water and the rough vegetables and seasoning. Cook slowly for at least 5 hours. Strain up and leave to stand until next day.

Remove all fat. Put stock back into a saucepan and boil until the quantity is so reduced as to become a thick glaze.

BACON AND MUSHROOM FLAN

4 oz mushrooms; 4 oz bacon; ½ oz butter; 2 oz grated cheese; 3 egg yolks; 1 gill cream; seasoning.

Line a deep flan ring with good short pastry. Beat egg and cheese together, add seasoning and cream.

Cut the mushrooms and bacon into dice and gently fry in the butter. Add this to the egg mixture and mix well. Fill the pastry case with the mixture and bake in a moderate oven for about ½ hour.

BLANQUETTE DE VEAU À L'ANCIENNE

For six people.

3 lb veal breast; 1 pint white stock; roughly chopped vegetables; bouquet garni; little butter and flour; 2 egg yolks; 2 tablespoons cream; chopped parsley; seasoning; ½ lb button mushrooms; ½ lb button onions.

Cut the veal into small pieces, blanch, cool and strain, then cook in the white stock and roughly chopped vegetables for 1½ hours.

Remove the meat and strain off the stock. Prepare a roux of butter and flour and gently add the stock. Boil for 2 or 3 minutes, add the previously cooked mushrooms and onions and replace the meat. Simmer for 5 minutes, and finally add the egg yolks and cream which should be blended together first. Do not allow to boil again. Sprinkle the parsley.

BRASCIOLETTE

For four people.

1 lb shin of beef; 1 lb lean steak; 3 oz white breadcrumbs; chopped parsley; a little stock; seasoning; 3 rashers of bacon.

Pass 1 lb raw beef twice through a mincer and then through a coarse sieve. Mix with a little chopped parsley, breadcrumbs and stock. Season.

Cut a 1 lb steak into slices 1½ inches wide. Flatten with a rolling pin. Cut a slice of bacon to the size of the steak and place on each piece. Add to this a good layer of the raw beef mixture, roll up and place side by side in a fireproof dish. Cover with greased paper and cook very slowly in the oven for 1 hour.

Serve with a good tomato sauce.

BOEUF À LA BOURGEOISE

4 lb lean topside of beef; ½ lb stoned olives; 5 large skinned and seeded tomatoes; tablespoon brandy; butter; seasoning.

Put a knob of butter in a stewpan over gentle heat. When the butter steams place in the beef (whole), brown well on both sides. Add salt and pepper. Pour over a good tablespoonful of brandy and flame this, replacing the saucepan lid immediately. Cook very slowly in the oven for 3 hours.

Cut the tomatoes in halves and cook in butter with seasoning and chopped parsley.

About ¼ hour before the meat is cooked, put in the tomatoes and olives.

Remove the meat, cut into slices and place on the serving dish. Garnish with the tomatoes, olives and pour over the juice from the meat.

PIÈCE DE BOEUF BOURGUIGNONNE

4 lb rump of beef; ½ pint brandy and red wine mixed; 1 pint brown stock; 1 large bouquet garni; ¼ lb mushroom peelings.

Garnish
Braised balls of cabbage; small cooked carrots and button onions; 6 small frankfurters.

Lard beef with larding fat or fat bacon, place in a deep dish with the brandy and red wine and seasoning and leave to pickle for 4 hours. During this time turn the meat twice.

Take up and dry the meat on a muslin. Brown on both sides in hot fat in a large stewpan, add the brown stock, pickle, mushroom peelings, bouquet garni and seasoning.

Cook in oven, with the lid on, for 3 ½ hours or until tender.

Take up meat and keep hot. Pass the liquor through a strainer, reduce in quantity and serve with the meat.

QUEUE DE BOEUF

1 oxtail; 12 small onions; about 18 cooked chestnuts; 1 pint red wine; blade of garlic; Julienne of bacon.

Cut the oxtail in sections and fry until well browned. Flour and fry again, add 1 pint of red wine, a blade of garlic and seasoning. Simmer gently for 4 hours.

Braise the onions and chestnuts for 1 hour.

Garnish the oxtail with the braised vegetables and Julienne of fried bacon.

CERVELLES CONNAUGHT

For four people.

2 sets of brains; butter; 1 oz flour; 1 teaspoon curry powder; a little chopped mango chutney; 3 tablespoons cream.

Wash and cleanse the brains. Melt a little butter in a saucepan, put in the brains, salt and pepper and cook very slowly for about ½ hour. Put aside to cool.

Make a sauce with a little butter, one tablespoon flour and curry powder mixed. Add a little chopped mango chutney and juice of the brains. Cook for 15 minutes, pass through a strainer and then add 3 tablespoons cream.

Cut the brains into slices, reheat in a greased covered dish in the oven. Place on serving dish and coat with boiling sauce.

CONCOMBRES INDIENNE

For six people.

2 cucumbers; 1 lb raw veal; 2 egg whites; 1 gill cream; 2 tablespoons white stock.

Remove the skin from 2 cucumbers, cut into 4 portions, cut again in halves lengthwise and remove the seeds. Blanch in salted water for 2 minutes. Allow to cool.

Mince 1 lb raw veal and pass through a sieve with 2 whites of eggs. Put into a basin with a gill of cream and beat well. Season. Fill the cucumber portions with this mixture and put into a well-greased dish with 2 tablespoons of white stock. Cover with greased paper and cook in the oven slowly for about 20 minutes.

Place the cucumber on to the serving dish, pour over a light curry sauce. Serve with boiled rice on a napkin.

CÔTELETTES BERGÈRE

6 cutlets (best end of neck of lamb); 6 slices of grilled ham; ½ lb button onions; egg and breadcrumbs; seasoning.

Trim and shorten cutlets. Egg and breadcrumb and cook in clarified butter. Dress in a circle alternately with slices of grilled ham.

Garnish with straw potatoes and button onions cooked in butter.

CÔTELETTES DE BOEUF RUSSE

For six people.

1½ lb beef steak; ½ pint sour cream; 2 oz butter; 3 small cooked beetroots; 3 tablespoons fresh cream; 3 onions; seasoning; nutmeg.

Put the beef steak through a mincing machine twice; put into a basin and mix in the sour cream a little at a time until a stiff paste is formed. Add a little oiled butter, nutmeg and seasoning. Shape into cutlets, flour well and cook slowly in clarified butter.

Garnish
Cut the beetroot into large dice, mix with fresh cream, and season. Cut onions into very thin rings, flour and fry in deep fat.

CÔTELETTES DE CHEVREUIL

Neck of venison; butter; cream; few drops of lemon juice and a little cherry juice; stoned cherries.

Cut as many cutlets as required, not too large. Melt some butter in a frying pan, cook the cutlets slowly for about 10 minutes turning only once. Remove the cutlets and place on a hot dish. Swill the frying pan with cream, add a few drops of lemon juice and a little cherry juice.

Garnish with stoned cooked cherries and pour over the sauce.

CÔTELETTES MAINTENON

For six people.

6 cutlets (best end of neck of lamb); 1 lb potatoes; ½ lb onions; little grated cheese; butter; seasoning.

Trim some of the fat off the cutlets and remove a little of the bone to shorten.

Peel and boil potatoes, fry the onions in some butter and pass all through a sieve together with seasoning.

Sauté the cutlets on one side only. Pile some potato and onion purée on the cooked side of each cutlet and sprinkle with a little grated cheese.

Move the cutlets into a buttered pan and fry for about 2 – 3 minutes.

Place under the grill in order to brown the purée.

ESCALOPES DE VEAU VIENNOISE

For four people.

Neck of veal (3 bones); white breadcrumbs; 1 lemon; anchovy fillets; 2 hard-boiled eggs and 1 uncooked egg; chopped parsley; seasoning.

Remove the meat from the bone and cut into thin slices. Mix a beaten egg with a little oiled butter and dip in the slices of meat, coat with breadcrumbs and fry lightly in butter. When cooked place on dish with a slice of lemon and anchovy fillet on each escallop. Garnish the side of the dish with sieved hard-boiled yolks and whites separately and chopped parsley.

Serve with good gravy.

CÔTELETTES DE MOUTON RÉFORME

For six people.

Cutlets as required; 3 oz breadcrumbs; 2 oz chopped cooked ham; 2 oz chopped cooked tongue; 2 oz chopped truffle; 2 egg yolks; 2 oz oiled butter; seasoning.

Trim the cutlets and make as neat as possible. Cook for 3 minutes one side only. Mix together the breadcrumbs, ham, tongue, oiled butter and truffle. Bind this mixture with the egg yolks and place in the form of a dome on the cooked side of each cutlet. With the raw side down put the cutlets in a pan and fry for 2 minutes. Afterwards place in the oven for a few minutes to cook the mixture.

Serve with Réforme sauce.

MÉDAILLONS DE VEAU PAPRIKA

Neck of veal; oiled butter; paprika pepper; 2 lb spinach; 2 tablespoons thick Béchamel sauce; 1 egg yolk; seasoning; few blanched leaves of spinach.

Cook the spinach in the normal way, but keep back a few large leaves which should be blanched only. Pass the spinach through a coarse sieve, mix with a little thick Béchamel sauce, egg yolk and seasoning. Place a tablespoon of this mixture into each blanched spinach leaf. Grease a fireproof dish well with butter and place in these subrics of spinach. Put the dish in the oven and cook slowly for 10 minutes under cover, to prevent hardening of the leaves.

Remove the bones from the neck of veal, and cut the meat into medium slices. Dip each slice in oiled butter, sprinkle well with paprika and fry them lightly in butter.

Arrange the veal on a dish with the subrics of spinach, and pour over a sauce made from cream mixed with juices in which the veal has been cooked.

MOUSSE DE JAMBON FROID

For six people.

2 lb cooked lean ham; 4 oz fresh tomato purée; paprika pepper; ½ pint cream; bare ½ oz gelatine; aspic jelly.

Mince ham, add tomato purée and a little paprika. Mix well and pass through a fine sieve. Put into a basin and stand on ice, add slowly ½ pint whipped cream and a little diluted gelatine. Leave to set. Turn out, cut into slices and place on a bed of chopped aspic jelly.

Serve with a salad of cooked peas or points of asparagus or celery mixed with cream.

NAVARIN DE MOUTON

For six people.

2 lb neck of mutton; ½ lb button onions; 1 lb small carrots; ½ lb small turnips; 1 cupful shelled peas; 1 lb small new potatoes; bouquet garni; 2 tablespoons flour.

Divide the meat into cutlets. Melt some butter in a stewpan and brown the meat very well. Take out meat, stir in the flour and allow to cook until the mixture leaves the sides of the stewpan. Add about 1 pint of water and bring to the boil. Replace the mutton, adding onions, bouquet garni and seasoning. Simmer for 1½ hours. When nearly cooked, brown some shaped turnips and carrots in butter and add to the stew, also a good handful of shelled peas. The potatoes can be put in with these vegetables.

Before serving, remove bouquet garni and sprinkle over some fresh chopped mint.

NOISETTES DE CHEVREUIL

Small neck of venison; ½ lb each button mushrooms and button onions; little chopped shallot.

Remove the meat from the bone and cut into thick round slices, about ¾ inch. Cook in butter with a little chopped shallot, turning only once. Remove the meat and swill the pan with a little lemon juice and the liquor in which the mushrooms and onions have been cooked.

Garnish with the mushrooms and onions and pour over the sauce.

PAUPIETTES DE VEAU ALGÉRIENNE

For four people.

1½ lb fillet of veal; white breadcrumbs; 1 lb small tomatoes; 1 red pepper; 1 egg yolk; oiled butter and seasoning; garlic.

Cut the veal into thin slices and bat them well. Season. Make a little forcemeat with breadcrumbs, 3 tomatoes skinned, seeded and chopped, 1 red pepper finely chopped, 1 small blade of garlic, egg yolk and oiled butter.

Spread some forcemeat on each slice of veal, roll up and braise for ¾ hour.

Serve with small croquettes of potatoes, skinned, seeded and cooked tomatoes.

TERRINE DE LIÈVRE

This dish should be prepared 2 days before needed.

1 hare; 4 bacon rashers; 3 tablespoons brandy; 2 tablespoons Madeira; few bay leaves; few peppercorns.

Remove all the meat from a hare, keeping the fillets of the back separate. Pass all the meat, except the fillets, twice through a mincer and then through a coarse sieve; season well, adding a few crushed peppercorns. Put some of the minced hare at the bottom of a tureen. Slice, and lard with fat bacon, the fillets from the back and place on top of the minced hare; now fill up with more of the mince. Pour over this the 3 tablespoons brandy and the 2 tablespoons of Madeira mixed with the blood of the hare, making sure the meat is well covered. Place on this a few bay leaves and rashers of bacon, put on the lid of the tureen and stand till next day.

Put some water into a baking tin and stand the tureen in. Cook for 1¼ hours. Take out the tureen and leave till next day.

Remove all fat and fill up with good aspic jelly made from the bones of the hare.

TOURNEDOS MEXICAINE

For six people.

2 lb fillet of beef; 6 large cooked mushrooms; 1 green and 1 red pimento; 4 tomatoes; blade of garlic.

Cut some small rounds about 1½ inches thick from the fillet of beef. Cook lightly in oiled butter.

Skin and seed tomato, sauté in butter with a very small amount of garlic and seasoning. Cook the mushrooms in the same manner but without garlic.

Place the tomato inside the mushroom with one fillet on each.

Seed, slice and fry lightly the pimentoes and serve as a garnish with the fillets.

TOURNEDOS MONTPENSIER

For six people.

6 short pastry tartlets; 2½ lb fillet of beef; 1 bundle of small asparagus; 6 pats of green butter.

Prepare 6 tartlets of short pastry. Cut off the points of the asparagus and cook in salted water, strain up and put in a little melted butter. Place a few of these tips in each tartlet.

Cut 6 small fillets from the beef in rounds, tie each with a piece of string to prevent spreading. Cook for 3 minutes each side in oiled butter, and then place one on each tartlet.

Make some green butter with chopped parsley, a little lemon juice and seasoning and place a pat on each fillet.

TOURNEDOS ROSSINI

For six people.

2½ lb fillet of beef; 4 oz natural foie gras; 1 very large truffle.

Cut some small rounds about 1½ inches thick from the fillet of beef. Tie round with string. Fry lightly in oiled butter about 3 minutes each side.

Cut 6 slices from the foie gras and 6 from the truffle, place one of each on the fillets having the truffle uppermost.

SAUCES

SAUCE ALBUFÉRA

½ pint Suprême sauce; 1 oz butter; 1 tinned pimento; 1 teaspoon meat extract.

Pass the butter and pimento through a fine sieve, add meat extract, Suprême sauce and serve very hot.

SAUCE ALLEMANDE

2 oz butter; 2 oz flour; 1 pint chicken stock; pepper and salt; 2 egg yolks; 2 tablespoons cream.

Make a roux with the butter and flour, add gradually the chicken stock, salt and pepper. Put the yolks of eggs into a basin, beat in the cream then whisk in the chicken and flour mixture.

SAUCE AURORE

Suprême sauce to which is added a little reduced tomato purée, salt, pepper and 1 oz of fresh butter. Serve very hot.

SAUCE BÉARNAISE

3 finely chopped shallots; black pepper; salt; tarragon vinegar; 4 egg yolks; 3 oz melted butter; tarragon leaves and chervil; ½ teaspoon melted glaze.

Put the chopped shallots, seasoning and about 3 tablespoons tarragon vinegar into a saucepan, cook until reduced to a third quantity. Remove from heat, add the yolks of eggs, oiled butter and whisk over a low heat until very thick. Pass through a strainer, add glaze, chopped tarragon leaves and chervil. This should be kept hot but without boiling until ready for serving.

BÉCHAMEL SAUCE

2 oz butter; 2 oz flour; ¾ pint milk; salt and pepper.

Melt the butter, stir in the flour and allow to cook over a very low heat for 10 minutes. Add milk gradually, stirring all the time, bring to the boil and boil for 20 minutes more. Add the seasoning.

Note
This is a foundation white sauce and can be used as a basis for many other sauces.

SAUCE BERCY

3 finely chopped shallots; ½ pint white wine; ¼ pint fish stock; salt and pepper; chopped parsley; 3oz butter; Béchamel sauce; 1 egg yolk.

Melt half the quantity of butter and fry the shallots lightly, add white wine, fish stock, salt and pepper. Cook for 20 minutes, or till reduced. Strain off and add 3 tablespoons Béchamel sauce. Replace over heat and whisk in the yolk of egg and remainder of butter.

Note
This can be used for meat dishes with meat glaze and a little chopped beef marrow in place of the fish stock.

SAUCE BIGARRADE

Rind of 1 orange; ¼ pint strong stock made from duck giblets; juice of 1 orange and 1 lemon; 1 oz butter; 1 teaspoon arrowroot.

Cut the rind of the orange into very thin strips and blanch in water. Strain off and put into a saucepan with the duck gravy, juice of the orange and lemon. Blend the butter with the arrowroot and whisk into the sauce. Season.

SAUCE BORDELAISE

3 finely chopped shallots; thyme; bay leaves; salt and pepper; ½ pint red wine; meat extract; 2 oz butter.

Fry the shallots in half the quantity of butter, add red wine, thyme, bay leaves, salt and pepper. Reduce to a third, strain, replace in saucepan and add the meat extract and remainder of the butter.

SAUCE BOURGUIGNONNE

3 finely chopped shallots; parsley stalks; little thyme; crumbled bay leaves; mushroom peelings; 3 oz butter; seasoning; ½ pint red wine; ½ oz flour.

Melt half the butter and fry the shallots; add the chopped parsley stalks, thyme, bay leaves, mushroom peelings and the red wine, pepper and salt. Cook slowly for ½ hour. Strain and put back again into a saucepan.

Work the flour in with the rest of the butter and whisk this into the sauce.

CHAUDFROID (WHITE)

¾ pint Béchamel sauce; ¼ pint cream; 1 oz gelatine.

Make ¾ pint Béchamel sauce hot. Dissolve the gelatine in a little cold milk, whisk well and add to the sauce. Remove from heat. When almost cold add the cream.

CHAUDFROID (BROWN)

¾ pint Béchamel sauce; 1 oz gelatine; meat extract; essence of truffle; concentrated game stock.

Make ¾ pint of Béchamel sauce, dissolve the gelatine in a little meat extract and whisk into the sauce. Add a little essence of truffle and concentrated game stock.

SAUCE CHORON

Make a good Béarnaise sauce and add 2 tablespoons tomato purée.

CUMBERLAND SAUCE

1 orange and 1 lemon; 3 shallots finely chopped; ½ lb redcurrant jelly; 1 wineglass port; 1 teaspoon ground ginger; salt and pepper; ½ teaspoon mixed mustard.

Cut a Julienne of orange and lemon rind and blanch in salted water with the chopped shallots. Strain off and put into a basin, add the juice of the orange and lemon, ground ginger, salt and pepper. Dissolve the redcurrant jelly, add the mustard and port wine, and whisk all together.

Serve cold with cold meats.

CURRY SAUCE

3 medium-sized onions; 2 oz butter; 1 dessertspoon curry powder; 1 blade of garlic; 1 oz flour; ½ pint meat stock; seasoning.

Dice the onions and fry in melted butter. Add the curry powder, garlic and flour and fry slowly until it leaves the sides of the pan. Gradually stir in the stock and cook for 30 minutes.

Strain and use as required.

SAUCE ESPAGNOLE

3 oz butter; 3 oz flour; 1 pint any kind of meat stock; ½ lb fresh tomatoes; ½ lb mushroom peelings; 2 chopped onions; 2 chopped carrots; sprig of thyme; 4 bay leaves; salt and pepper.

Melt the butter in a saucepan, add the flour and fry slowly until it is light brown. Add the stock, bring to the boil and whisk well. Cut the tomatoes in half and add to the sauce with the mushroom peelings, chopped onions, chopped carrots, thyme and bay leaves, salt and pepper. Cook very slowly for 2 hours. Put through a very fine strainer.

Note
This is the foundation of any brown sauce.

SAUCE HOLLANDAISE

4 egg yolks; 4 oz melted butter; juice of 1 lemon; 3 tablespoons vinegar; 4 crushed peppercorns; 1 tablespoon cold water.

Reduce the vinegar in a saucepan with the peppercorns. Remove from heat. Gradually stir in the yolks of eggs and half the quantity of melted butter, lemon juice, cold water, salt. Whisk vigorously until the mixture thickens, then add the remainder of the butter. This sauce must not be boiled and requires an even heat all through the cooking.

HORSERADISH SAUCE

3 oz grated horseradish; 1 gill cream; 1 level teaspoon mixed mustard; salt; pinch of sugar; 2 tablespoons vinegar; very little pepper.

Grate the horseradish into a basin, add the mustard, sugar, pepper, salt and vinegar. Whip the cream separately and add to the horseradish. Serve very cold.

MADEIRA SAUCE

1 gill Espagnole sauce; 1 teaspoon meat extract; 1 very finely chopped truffle; 3 tablespoons Madeira; 1 tablespoon truffle essence.

Add the meat extract to the Espagnole sauce and cook for 20 minutes, then add the chopped truffle, truffle essence and finally the Madeira.

MAYONNAISE

2 egg yolks; 1 tablespoon malt vinegar; 1 tablespoon tarragon vinegar; salt and pepper; pinch of sugar; ½ teaspoon mixed mustard; ½ pint olive oil.

Put the egg yolks in a basin, add salt, pepper, mixed mustard and sugar. Using a whisk, gradually add the vinegar then the oil drop by drop. Lastly whisk in 1 tablespoon boiling water.

MINT SAUCE

2 tablespoons mint; 1 tablespoon caster sugar; ½ gill vinegar; 1 tablespoon boiling water; 2 tablespoons redcurrant jelly; salt.

Wash and chop the mint very finely together with the sugar. Add the boiling water. Dissolve the redcurrant jelly in the vinegar and add to the mint.

SAUCE MORNAY

½ pint Béchamel sauce; 4 oz grated Parmesan and Gruyère cheese mixed; 1 oz butter; 2 tablespoons cream; pinch of cayenne.

Add the grated cheese, butter, cream and cayenne to the Béchamel sauce.

SAUCE NANTUA

1 head or shell of a cooked lobster; 2 onions; 2 carrots; ½ lb fresh tomatoes; parsley stalks; ½ pint white wine; 1 tablespoon brandy; 2 egg yolks; ½ gill cream; 2 oz butter; seasoning.

Chop up the onions, carrots and parsley stalks and fry in butter; season. Add the crushed shell of a lobster and the tablespoon of brandy. Set alight and cover immediately.

Add white wine and tomatoes roughly cut. Cook slowly for 1 hour. Pass through a fine sieve, put back into a saucepan and bring to the boil. Put the yolks of eggs into a basin, mix in the cream then pour in the boiling sauce; whisk well and keep hot.

SAUCE NORMANDE

3 oz butter; 2 oz flour; ½ pint fish stock; ¼ lb mushroom peelings; salt and pepper; 2 egg yolks; 4 tablespoons cream.

Melt 2 oz of the butter in a saucepan, add the flour, stir in slowly the fish stock, seasoning and mushroom peelings. Cook for 20 minutes. Strain and reheat. Put the yolks of eggs in a basin with the cream and whisk in the boiling sauce. Replace in a saucepan, add the remainder of the butter and keep hot.

SAUCE PIQUANTE

4 finely chopped shallots; 4 tablespoons vinegar; ½ pint Espagnole sauce; 4 chopped gherkins; 1 teaspoon meat extract; chopped tarragon and chervil; black pepper.

Put the vinegar into a saucepan with the chopped shallots and black pepper, reduce to half the amount, add the Espagnole sauce and the meat extract. Cook for 15 minutes, strain and just before serving add the chopped gherkin, tarragon and chervil.

SAUCE POIVRADE

2 onions; 2 carrots; green part of celery; sprig of thyme; 3 bay leaves; parsley stalks; 2 tablespoons vinegar; 3 tablespoons strong gravy or 1 tablespoon meat extract; 3 tablespoons olive oil; trimmings from game or hare.

Chop up all vegetables and fry in the oil, add the vinegar, strong gravy and game trimmings. Cook for 30 minutes. Pass through a very fine sieve. Reheat.

SAUCE PROVENÇALE

½ pint Espagnole sauce; ½ lb tomatoes; parsley stalks; 1 onion chopped finely; 3 tablespoons oil; blade of garlic; pinch of sugar.

Cut up the tomatoes and fry in the oil with a blade of garlic, parsley stalks, pinch of sugar and chopped onion. Fry well for 10 minutes. Add the Espagnole sauce, cook for 15 minutes, strain and add a little chopped parsley.

SAUCE RAVIGOTTE

1 gill olive oil; 3 tablespoons vinegar; salt and pepper; 1 oz chopped capers; 1 oz chopped tarragon, chervil and parsley mixed; 1 tablespoon very finely chopped shallot.

Whisk oil and vinegar together until quite thick, then add the rest of the ingredients.

Keep very cool.

SAUCE RÉFORME

½ pint Poivrade sauce; 2 tablespoons strong meat gravy; 1 wineglass of port; 2 hard-boiled egg whites; 3 gherkins; salt and black pepper; 3 mushrooms; 2 truffles; 2 slices of cooked tongue.

Cut the whites of eggs, gherkins, cooked mushrooms, truffle, and tongue into very thin strips and add to the Poivrade sauce.

Stir in the port wine and keep hot.

SAUCE SOUBISE

1 oz butter; 1 onion; 1 tablespoon flour; ½ pint milk; pepper and salt; 1 tablespoon cream.

Chop the onion very fine and fry in the butter, add the flour, seasoning and fry again for 5 minutes without colouring. Stir in the milk and cook slowly for ¾ hour. Strain and add the cream.

SAUCE SUPRÊME

2 oz butter; 2 oz flour; ¾ pint chicken stock; salt and pepper; 1 tablespoon juice from cooked mushrooms; 2 egg yolks; ½ gill cream.

Melt the butter in a saucepan, add the flour and seasoning. Whisk in the chicken stock, and the mushroom liquor and cook slowly for 15 minutes. Put the yolks of eggs into a basin with the cream, then whisk in the boiling sauce.

SAUCE TARTARE

½ pint mayonnaise; 2 hard-boiled egg yolks; finely chopped tarragon, chervil and chives; 1 very small shallot, finely chopped.

Pass the egg yolks through a sieve and add to the mayonnaise with the chopped tarragon, chervil, chives and shallot. Serve very cold.

TOMATO SAUCE

1 lb tomatoes; 3 chopped shallots; sprig of thyme; parsley stalks; pepper and salt; 1 teaspoon sugar; 3 tablespoons olive oil; 1 blade of garlic.

Put the oil into a saucepan and fry the shallots; add the thyme, parsley stalks, garlic, seasoning and sugar. Cut the tomatoes up roughly and add to the rest. Stir well and cook slowly for ½ hour. Pass through a fine sieve, reheat and add a small knob of butter.

SAUCE VERTE

½ pint mayonnaise; few leaves of spinach; tarragon leaves and chervil; watercress and parsley.

Blanch the spinach, watercress and herbs in salted water. Strain well, pass through a fine sieve and add to the mayonnaise. Serve very cold.

SAUCE VILLEROY

½ pint Allemande sauce; 1 tablespoon juice extracted from undercooked ham; 1 tablespoon truffle essence.

Add the ham juice and truffle essence to the Allemande sauce.

Note
This sauce is used more as a coating for chicken and cutlets.

SALADS

ARTICHOKE SALAD

6 globe artichokes; asparagus points (cooked); chopped salted almonds; juice of 2 lemons; ¼ pint cream; seasoning; chopped parsley.

Boil the artichokes in salted water for ½ hour. Remove the leaves. Cut the artichoke bottoms into pieces and place in a salad bowl with the same amount of asparagus points. Make a dressing with the cream, lemon juice, seasoning and chopped almonds. Pour over the salad and sprinkle with chopped parsley.

BROAD BEAN SALAD

1 lb very young cooked broad beans.

Make a dressing with 2 tablespoons oil, 1 tablespoon vinegar, a little mixed mustard, salt and pepper, a little chopped chives and about 3 leaves of fresh sage chopped very finely.

Put the beans in a salad bowl and mix well with the dressing.

Allow to stand for at least an hour before serving.

CELERY, BEETROOT AND APPLE SALAD

1 large head of celery; 1 large cooked beetroot; 2 large dessert apples; 4 tablespoons cream; ½ oz sugar; seasoning; 1 tablespoon vinegar; ½ teaspoon mixed mustard.

Cut the celery into small strips, wash in cold water and dry. Peel, core and cut into squares the dessert apples and place in cold salted water to keep crisp until ready for use.

Put the cream into a basin with the sugar, seasoning, vinegar and mustard, mix together.

Strain off water from apples, cut the beetroot into dice and mix in with the dressing and the celery.

COLESLAW

2 egg yolks; salt, pepper; mixed mustard; 3 tablespoons cream; 1 tablespoon vinegar; 3 tablespoons Béchamel sauce; 1 medium white cabbage.

Cut up the cabbage into Julienne and put into cold water to crisp.

Make a dressing by putting the yolks of eggs into a basin over hot water, add the seasoning, mustard, cream, vinegar and stir well until it thickens. Add the Béchamel sauce, then remove from heat and leave until cold. Strain off the cabbage and dry on a muslin and mix in with the dressing.

Serve very cold.

CUCUMBER AND TOMATO SALAD

Cucumber; tomatoes; oil; vinegar; seasoning and chopped tarragon.

Cut the cucumber into large dice without removing the skin, put into a dish, salt well and leave to stand for ½ hour.

Skin and seed the tomatoes and cut into dice, season well and add a pinch of sugar. Mix them with a dressing of 2 tablespoons oil and 1 tablespoon vinegar and chopped tarragon. Strain the water off the cucumber and mix in with the tomato and dressing.

Serve very cold.

FRENCH BEAN SALAD

Boil the quantity of beans required and cut into halves if too long. Allow to get cold. Make a dressing with 3 tablespoons oil, 2 tablespoons vinegar, seasoning, 1 teaspoon chopped chives and parsley. Toss the beans in this dressing and serve very cold.

MIMOSA SALAD

Quarters of lettuce hearts; quarters of orange; cream; lemon juice; salt; hard-boiled egg yolk; chopped parsley.

Arrange the lettuce and orange quarters in a bowl. Make a dressing by mixing cream with lemon juice and adding seasoning. Pour over the salad and sprinkle with the yolk of hard-boiled egg passed through a sieve, and chopped parsley.

POTATO SALAD

Boil some potatoes in their skins in salted water. Whilst still hot skin and cut into thin slices. Put into a basin and mix with oil, vinegar, chopped chives and seasoning. Add a little mixed mustard.

Serve cold.

POTATO SALAD WITH MAYONNAISE

Boil some good firm potatoes in their skins in salted water. Skin and cut into slices whilst they are still hot. Toss them in mixed oil and vinegar and leave until quite cold. Make a thick mayonnaise and mix in the potato with a little chopped chives and parsley.

Serve very cold.

TOMATO SALAD

1 lb tomatoes; sugar and seasoning.

Skin and seed the tomatoes, cut into quarters then halve again. Put into a dish with sugar and seasoning.

Dressing

4 tablespoons oil; 1 tablespoon tarragon vinegar; 1 tablespoon chilli vinegar; 1 teaspoon mixed mustard; chopped chives and tarragon leaves.

Put the oil into a basin, mix in the vinegars, mustard, chopped chives and tarragon.

Put the tomatoes into the dressing and leave to stand for 2 hours before serving.

SALADE DURRAND

Celery; cooked potatoes; red part of cooked tongue; tomatoes, skinned and seeded; cooked asparagus points; mayonnaise; cream.

Cut the celery, potatoes, tongue and tomatoes into large strips. Dilute the mayonnaise with a little cream, season and mix all together.

Serve very cold.

SALADE SUÉDOISE

2 large apples; 4 large cooked potatoes; 3 gherkins; ½ cucumber; 4 stoned prunes; 4 skinned and seeded tomatoes; 3 hard-boiled egg whites; ½ pint mayonnaise; 2 tablespoons cream; seasoning.

Cut into dice the apples, potatoes and cucumber. Julienne the prunes, gherkins and seeded tomatoes and whites of hard- boiled eggs. Mix all well together in the mayonnaise, to which a little cream has been added.

Serve in a bowl with lettuce leaves around.

VEGETABLES

ARTICHAUTS

Artichokes; Duxelle; chopped ham; shallots; breadcrumbs; mixed vegetables; white wine; seasoning.

Trim and blanch globe artichokes, remove the centres and fill with Duxelle preparation mixed with chopped ham. Braise in a casserole dish on a bed of mixed vegetables and a little white wine for 1 hour. Remove the artichokes and make a sauce with the liquor.

Duxelle
Chopped shallot and mushrooms seasoned and fried in butter with a little breadcrumbs added.

ARTICHAUTS HOLLANDAISE

Artichoke leaves; Hollandaise sauce.

Trim off the points of the artichoke leaves. Cook for ½ hour in salted boiling water and serve with Hollandaise sauce.

AUBERGINES FRITES

Aubergines; flour; egg; olive oil.

Peel the aubergines and cut into slices. Make a batter of flour, salt, egg, water and a little olive oil. Dip the slices of aubergine into the batter and fry in deep fat.

CAROTTES À LA CRÈME

Carrots; 1 oz butter; cream; parsley; seasoning.

Cut the carrots into small shapes and cook in a very little water to which a pinch of salt has been added. Add about 1 oz of butter and allow to cook slowly until nearly all the liquor is absorbed, then add a little cream and chopped parsley.

CÉLERI AU JUS

Celery; roughly chopped vegetables; bouquet garni; bacon; stock; butter; seasoning.

Wash the hearts of celery, trim the leaves and cut in half lengthwise. Cook in boiling salted water for 5 minutes. Take up. Prepare a casserole with a bed of roughly chopped vegetables, a good bouquet garni, strips of bacon and a pint of stock. Place in the hearts of celery, cover, and cook in the oven for 1 hour. Remove celery and keep hot. Strain off the liquor from the casserole and reduce to about half a gill, add a lump of butter and pour this over the celery before serving.

CHICORY

Chicory; butter; parsley; lemon; seasoning.

Wash and boil the chicory whole in salted water for 5 minutes. Strain and put into a saucepan with plenty of butter, salt and pepper. Turn now and again to prevent them browning. Remove from saucepan, place on a hot dish and sprinkle with chopped parsley and a squeeze of lemon before serving.

CHOUX BRAISÉS

Cabbage; carrots; onions; turnips; bouquet garni; 1 pint stock.

Wash the cabbage and blanch in salted boiling water. Strain.

Butter a saucepan and make a bed of carrots, onions, turnips and a bouquet garni. Place the cabbage on this and add about 1 pint of any kind of stock. Season and cook till tender. Remove the cabbage, cut in four and serve.

CHOUX FARCIS

Savoy cabbage; seasoned sausage meat; mixed vegetables.

Take some good leaves of a savoy cabbage and blanch them in salted water. Strain off liquid. Spread out the leaves one on top of the other, place in the centre of each a ball of seasoned sausage meat. Roll up leaves and braise for 1 hour on a bed of mixed vegetables. Serve with strong meat gravy.

CHOUX ROUGE FLAMANDE

Red cabbage; vinegar; seasoning; apples; brown sugar; bacon.

Cut a red cabbage into quarters and remove all stalk. Shred finely and cook in a casserole with butter, a little vinegar, salt and pepper. When almost cooked, add 3 chopped apples, brown sugar and a little Julienne of bacon. Finish cooking, taking in all about 2 hours.

CHOUXFLEUR MILANAISE

Cauliflower; Parmesan cheese; butter.

Break off some branches of cauliflower and cook them for 10 minutes in salted boiling water. Take up and dry on a muslin.

Butter a gratin dish and lay the cauliflower in, sprinkle well with cheese, pour round melted butter and put in the oven to brown.

CROQUETTES DE POMMES DE TERRE

6 medium-sized potatoes; 2 egg yolks; butter; seasoning; breadcrumbs.

Boil the potatoes in their skins, strain, peel and pass them through a sieve. Add 2 yolks of eggs, a good size knob of butter, salt, pepper and beat them well. Leave to cool and then shape as required. Flour them and dip into well-beaten egg. Roll in breadcrumbs and fry in deep fat.

DUCHESS POTATOES

6 medium-sized potatoes; 2 egg yolks; butter; seasoning.

Bake the potatoes in their skins until soft. Cut in half and take out the potato with a spoon, pass through a sieve, add yolks of eggs, butter, seasoning and beat well.

Note
This is a basis for use in various forms: borders, shapes and piping.

ENDIVES AU FROMAGE

Endives; melted butter; grated Parmesan cheese.

Wash and blanch the endives in salted water. Strain up and put the hearts into a buttered dish, pour over melted butter and a good sprinkling of grated cheese. Place in oven for 15 minutes to finish cooking.

HARICOTS VERTS À LA CRÈME

French beans; butter; cream; shallot; pepper.

Wash, top and tail the beans and place in boiling salted water, cook for 5 minutes.

Melt a good lump of butter in a saucepan, add a cupful of cream, a little finely chopped shallot and pepper. Add the beans to this and continue cooking until tender.

MACÉDOINE DE LÉGUMES

Carrots; turnips; button onions; butter; sugar.

Scrape a bundle of young carrots and turnips, peel 2 dozen button onions and place them all in a saucepan with about 2 oz of butter and about 1 teaspoonful of sugar. Brown them very lightly turning with a wooden spoon.

Cover with water and cook for ¾ hour. Strain off the liquid, add a little butter and serve with any kind of braised meat.

NAVETS AU BEURRE

Turnips; butter; cream; black pepper.

Peel and shape some turnips in large olives. Cook in boiling salted water for 5 minutes. Take up and put into another saucepan with melted butter, a little cream and black pepper.

PETITS POIS À LA FRANÇAISE

Peas; butter; sugar; button onions; parsley.

Shell the peas and put into a saucepan with 1½ oz butter, 1 tablespoon sugar, and a cup of water to every quart of shelled peas. Put over a gentle heat and mix lightly with a wooden spoon. Add a small bouquet of parsley, salt and pepper and a little more butter. Peel a dozen small onions, add to the peas and allow to cook slowly for 1 hour. Remove the parsley before serving.

PETITS POIS À LA PARISIENNE

Peas; button onions; cabbage lettuce; butter; sugar.

Melt about 1½ oz butter in a pan and put in a quart of shelled peas with a little salt. Mix lightly together with a wooden spoon, add 12 small onions, a shredded cabbage lettuce and allow to cook for an hour. No water is necessary as the lettuce will moisten the peas sufficiently. Add more butter and a little sugar and serve.

POMMES DE TERRE ALLUMETTES

Potatoes; salt.

Wash and peel potatoes and cut into thin matches. Dry very well and fry in deep fat. At the last moment sprinkle with salt.

POMMES DE TERRE ANNA

Potatoes; fresh butter.

Peel some potatoes and cut into very thin rounds the size of a florin. Wash in salted water and dry very well in a cloth. Well butter an omelette pan, place a layer of potatoes on the bottom, cover with oiled butter, pepper and salt. Repeat these layers until the pan is full and cook in a medium oven until brown. Remove from the oven, turn out and cut in slices or serve whole in a dish.

POMMES DE TERRE BOULANGÈRE

Potatoes; onions; stock.

Thinly slice some onions and cook in butter without colouring. Peel and slice potatoes, place on top of the onions, season, cover with a little stock of any kind and cook in the oven. Keep the pan covered with a lid whilst in the oven.

POMMES DE TERRE DAUPHINE

Duchess potatoes; choux pastry; egg white; breadcrumbs.

2 parts Duchess potatoes and 1 part choux pastry (unsweetened). Beat well together and form in small cork shapes. Egg, breadcrumb and fry in deep fat.

Alternatively, take small dessertspoonfuls of the mixture and drop in boiling fat.

POMMES DE TERRE GRENOBLE

Potatoes; garlic; butter; milk.

Peel and cut potatoes into thin round slices. Well butter a round fireproof dish, put in some of the potatoes, salt, pepper and 2 small blades of garlic. Dot with small knobs of butter. Arrange another layer of potatoes and butter, cover with milk and cook slowly in the oven until brown on top.

POMMES DE TERRE AU LAIT

Potatoes; milk; butter; garlic; parsley.

Peel and cut some potatoes into shapes of half moons. Blanch in salted water, strain up and put them into a saucepan with a little milk and butter, very small blade of garlic and chopped parsley. Simmer gently until soft.

POMMES DE TERRE AU LARD

Potatoes; shallots; rashers of bacon; black pepper.

Partly boil some potatoes in their skin in salted water. Remove from water and leave till cold. Peel off skins and cut into slices ¼ inch thick. Chop and fry 2 or 3 shallots with rashers of bacon cut into Julienne, and add the potatoes to this with a little black pepper. Keep tossing the potatoes over a slow heat till cooked.

POMMES DE TERRE MAÎTRE D'HÔTEL

Potatoes; butter; chopped parsley; seasoning.

Wash and boil the potatoes in their skins. Peel and cut into slices about a ¼ inch thick.

Melt some butter in a small saucepan, add a little chopped parsley, salt and pepper and pour over the potatoes.

POMMES DE TERRE NATURE AU BEURRE

Potatoes; butter.

Cut potatoes into the shape of large olives, put into a saucepan with a little water and small amount of salt. Add butter, about 2 oz to ½ pint of water. Cook very slowly until the potatoes almost absorb the liquor.

POMMES DE TERRE NORMANDE

Potatoes; onions; leek; butter; milk; breadcrumbs.

Peel and slice 6 medium-sized potatoes, 2 onions and the white part of a leek. Melt 2 oz of butter and cook all together, season well, add about ½ pint of milk and transfer to a fireproof dish to finish cooking in the oven. Finally sprinkle over some breadcrumbs which have been browned in butter.

POMMES DE TERRE SABLÉES

Potatoes; butter; Parmesan cheese; parsley.

Peel and cut some large potatoes into discs about ¾ inch in diameter. Blanch in salted water, strain and dry. Melt some butter in a pan, put in the potatoes and keep shaking them until they begin to colour. Sprinkle over some grated cheese mixed with chopped parsley and finish cooking.

POMMES DE TERRE SAUTÉES

Potatoes; parsley; butter.

Wash as many potatoes as required and boil them in their skins. When cooked remove skin. Melt some butter in a frying pan, cut the potatoes into round slices into the pan. Turn carefully with a palette knife and when slightly brown sprinkle with salt and chopped parsley.

PURÉE OF SPINACH

2 lb spinach; butter; 2 tablespoons cream; seasoning.

After washing the spinach well, place it in a saucepan of boiling salted water and cook for 5 minutes. Strain off the liquid until the spinach is as dry as possible. Pass through a fine wire sieve. Melt the butter in a saucepan, add the spinach purée, salt and pepper, and cook slowly for 5 minutes. Add the cream.

Note
If this purée is used for fish dishes, 1 oz of grated Parmesan cheese should be added with the cream.

SALSIFIS À LA CRÈME

Salsify; vinegar; flour; Béchamel sauce.

Scrape the salsify and immediately place in cold water with a little vinegar to preserve the colour.

Mix a tablespoonful of flour with a little cold water in a basin and add a good pint and a half of boiling water. Pour this back into a saucepan, add the salsify – cut into lengths – and boil until cooked. Strain and serve with a Béchamel sauce. Salsify can also be served with melted butter, to which has been added brown breadcrumbs, and cream.

PUDDINGS

ALEXANDER PUDDING

For four people.

4 oz butter; 4 oz sugar; 8 oz white breadcrumbs; 3 eggs; grated rind and juice of lemon; 1 tablespoon marmalade.

Cream the butter and sugar, beat in the egg yolks and add the breadcrumbs, rind and juice of the lemon and 1 tablespoonful of marmalade. Mix well and lastly add the 3 whites of egg whipped to a stiff froth.

Steam in a buttered basin for 1 hour.

AMBER PUDDING

For six people.

8 oz grated suet; 8 oz breadcrumbs; 6 oz caster sugar; 8 oz apricot jam; grated rind of 1 lemon; 4 eggs.

Mix together the suet, breadcrumbs, sugar, and grate in the rind of 1 lemon. Add the apricot jam and beat in 4 yolks of eggs. Mix all well together and finally add the whipped whites of egg.

Steam for 3 hours.

Serve with hot apricot jam sauce.

APPLES IN SYRUP

Dessert apples; ½ lb sugar; 1 pint water; lemon rind cut in strips; 1 cinnamon stick; 3 cloves; rum.

Peel and core the apples which should be small and of the same size.

Put sugar and water into a saucepan and bring to the boil, add lemon rind cut into strips, cinnamon stick and cloves. Boil for 5 minutes. Place the apples in this syrup and leave them to poach but not boil. When they are soft, remove from the heat and set aside to absorb as much juice as possible. Take up and arrange the apples in a fireproof dish, pour over about 4 tablespoons of warm rum, set alight and serve whilst burning.

BAKED APPLE PUDDING

For six people.

3 lb cooking apples; 14 oz breadcrumbs; 12 oz grated suet; 6 oz flour; 6 oz caster sugar; grated lemon rind; knobs of butter.

Peel, core and make a purée of the apple, with lemon rind. Mix well the breadcrumbs, suet, sugar and flour. Butter a pie dish and cover the bottom with a layer of the breadcrumb mixture, next a layer of the apple purée and so on until all is used making the top layer one of breadcrumbs.

Bake slowly for 1½ hours.

BABA AU RHUM

1 lb plain flour; 1 oz yeast; 3 oz sugar; 6 oz sultanas; 3 oz butter; 7 eggs; ¾ pint milk; pinch of salt; apricot jam; ½ lb sugar, ½ pint water, 6 tablespoons of rum for syrup.

Warm ¼ pint of milk and place in a basin with the yeast, add 1 oz of the sugar and about a quarter of the flour. Mix into a light dough and cover with the remainder of the flour and sugar. Cover the basin with a cloth and leave in a warm place for 20 minutes. By this time the dough should have broken through the covering of flour and sugar. Work in the eggs one at a time with the remainder of the milk and the 3 oz of butter. Knead for about 10 minutes then add the sultanas. Well grease 2 moulds, half fill with the mixture and leave to stand for ¾ of an hour. Bake in a moderate oven for ¾ of an hour to an hour.

Turn out of the moulds, mask over with apricot jam.

Make a syrup by placing the ½ lb sugar and ¼ pint of water together in a saucepan. Boil for 10 minutes, remove from heat and add the rum. Spoon the syrup over the cakes until all the syrup has been absorbed.

Serve hot or cold.

BEIGNETS

½ lb choux pastry; 1 oz sugar; vanilla essence; ½ lb raspberry jam.

Mix the choux pastry with the sugar and a few drops of vanilla essence. Drop a spoonful of the mixture into very hot, but not boiling, deep fat. Fry slowly until a golden brown. Place the beignets on some kitchen paper to remove any surplus grease.

Make the raspberry jam hot in a saucepan and serve with the beignets.

BOODLES ORANGE FOOL

For six people.

6 sponge cakes; 4 oranges; 2 lemons; ¾ pint cream; sugar to taste.

Cut up sponge cakes lengthwise in slices and place in a glass dish.

Put in a basin the grated rind of lemon and 2 oranges and the juice of all the fruit. Mix with the cream and sugar to taste. Pour all over the sponge cakes and allow to stand for 6 hours before serving.

BROWN BREAD PUDDING

For six people.

8 oz butter; 8 oz caster sugar; 7 oz brown breadcrumbs; 4 eggs; few drops vanilla essence; raspberry jam for sauce.

Cream the butter and sugar together until white and fluffy, add the brown breadcrumbs and vanilla essence. Separate the eggs and add the yolks to the mixture; beat well. Whip the whites until very stiff and fold in.

Butter a charlotte mould, pour in the mixture and steam for 1 hour. Serve with hot raspberry jam sauce.

CLAFOUTIS

For six people.

1 lb flour; 4 eggs; 2 oz caster sugar; 1 pint milk; 1 lb black cherries; 2 liqueur glasses of brandy; pinch of salt.

Sift the flour into a bowl with the salt. Break the eggs into flour and mix into a smooth paste, gradually adding the milk and sugar. Remove the stones from the cherries, add these to the paste with the brandy.

Well butter a shallow dish, put in the mixture and bake in the oven for ½ hour.

Sprinkle with icing sugar before serving.

CRÈME D'ABRICOTS

For six people.

1 tin apricots; 2 lemons; 4 oz sugar; ½ oz gelatine; ½ pint whipped cream; 2 oz chopped almonds.

Put the apricots in a saucepan with the grated rind of 2 lemons and sugar.

Boil slowly for 10 minutes, then pass through a fine sieve.

Dissolve the gelatine in a little of the purée and add to the mixture with the whipped cream and chopped almonds.

Serve very cold in a glass dish.

CRÊPES FLAMBÉES

For six people.

4 eggs; 8 oz flour; 2 oz sugar; pinch of salt; 1 gill cream; 1 oz oiled butter; 1 tablespoon brandy; bare ½ pint milk.

Beat together the eggs and milk, add flour, salt and sugar, oiled butter, and cream. Allow to stand for ½ hour.

Make pancakes in the usual way from this batter and when ready to serve pour over hot brandy and set alight.

CRÊPES FRANÇAISES

For four people.

2 oz butter; 2 oz sugar; 2 oz flour; 2 eggs; ½ pint milk; apricot jam.

Cream butter and sugar, add flour and the yolks of the eggs and milk. Whip the whites to a stiff froth and add to the mixture.

Butter 6 saucers, place some of the mixture on each saucer and bake for 20 minutes in a moderate oven.

Remove from saucers to hot dish and serve with sieved hot jam sauce.

CRÊPES SUZETTE

1 pint milk; 3 eggs; 8 oz flour; 3 oz butter; pinch of salt.

Sauce
6 lumps of sugar; 2 oranges; 3 tablespoons curaçao; 2 oz butter; 1 tablespoon brandy.

Make a batter with the milk, flour and eggs and a pinch of salt. Beat well and allow to stand for 1 hour or more if possible.

Have the butter melted ready and well grease the frying pan before cooking each pancake. Only a small amount of batter should be poured into the pan as the pancakes should be kept very thin. Lightly brown both sides, remove from pan and fold and keep hot.

Sauce mixture
Rub the sugar on to the rind of the oranges to extract all the zest and place in a saucepan. Add the juice of the oranges, butter, curaçao and brandy. Bring to the boil.

Place the pancakes in a hot dish and pour over the boiling sauce. Serve at once.

GÂTEAU FRANCILLON

For six people.

1 large round sponge cake; ½ pint fresh strawberry pulp; ¾ pint fresh cream; 4 oz caster sugar.

Scoop out the inside of the sponge cake, turn upside down and mask over with a thin meringue. Put into a cool oven to dry off. Fill the shell with strawberry ice cream. Serve with the meringue side uppermost.

Serve small fresh strawberries in a syrup separately.

Strawberry ice cream
Whip the cream until stiff, add the strawberry pulp and sugar and freeze until hard.

GÂTEAU DE POMME SUISSE

For six people.

2 lb cooking apples; 8 oz butter; 12 oz flour; 4 oz sugar; 2 eggs; pinch of salt; bare ½ oz yeast; 2 tablespoons milk; 4 oz crushed ratafia biscuits; 4 oz mixed currants, sultanas and chopped citron peel; apricot jam.

Peel and cut apples into slices and sauté in 4 oz of the butter, add the sugar when apples are soft.

Make a pastry as follows: Dissolve the yeast in the milk. Rub the butter into the flour, add the dissolved yeast and salt. Work in the eggs to form a pastry and roll out to oblong shape. Leave to prove for 1 hour.

Spread on the crushed ratafia biscuits, currants, sultanas and peel; then cover all with the sauté apple mixture. Twist up some pieces of the pastry and criss-cross the top.

Bake in the oven for 1 hour.

Mask over with a little apricot jam.

GINGER CREAM

For six people.

¾ pint whipped cream; 3 oz preserved ginger; ½ oz ground ginger; ½ oz gelatine; 1 gill milk; 3 egg yolks; 4 oz sugar.

Dissolve the gelatine and dry ginger in the milk and put into a basin with the 3 egg yolks and sugar and beat over hot water until it thickens. Remove from heat and allow to cool. Cut up the preserved ginger into small dice and add. Lastly whip the cream and stir in the mixture.

GLACÉ MOSCOVITE

For four people.

1½ lb fresh blackcurrants; 5 oz caster sugar; ¾ pint whipped cream; 6 fresh green figs.

Pass the blackcurrants and sugar through a hair sieve; add the whipped cream, and freeze.

Cook the figs in a syrup for 5 minutes and cool. Serve the figs around the heaped ice cream.

GUARDS PUDDING

For six people.

3 oz breadcrumbs; 2 oz sugar; 2 oz butter (oiled); 3 oz strawberry jam; 3 eggs; 1 saltspoon bicarbonate of soda.

Mix all dry ingredients together in a basin with the jam, beat in the eggs, and lastly sift in the bicarbonate of soda.

Steam for 2 hours in a buttered basin and serve with either strawberry or raspberry jam sauce.

INDIAN PUDDING

For four people.

3 oz butter; 2 oz flour; ¼ pint milk; 3 oz caster sugar; 3 oz chopped preserved ginger; 3 eggs; 1 teaspoon powdered ginger.

Line a mould with caramel by melting sugar in a pan till brown and then running it into the bottom of the warm mould and round the sides.

Melt the butter in a saucepan, add the flour and dry ginger. Add the milk, stir well and cook until it thickens. Add the sugar and preserved ginger, remove from heat, add the yolks of eggs and lastly the whites of eggs whipped to a stiff froth.

Pour the mixture into the mould, leaving sufficient room for rising. Steam for 2 hours.

Serve with hot golden syrup to which has been added a little dry ginger.

KAISER SCHMARN

For four people.

8 oz flour; ½ pint cream; little sugar; 4 eggs; few sultanas; salt; ½ oz powdered cinnamon; raspberry sauce and whipped cream.

Beat cream and yolks of eggs together, add salt, flour, sultanas and sugar. Fold in 4 stiffly whipped whites of egg. Cook for 20 minutes in a frying pan in a medium oven. When cooked remove from oven and pull apart with 2 forks into crumble. Mix all with sugar and powdered cinnamon and serve very hot.

Serve with raspberry sauce and whipped cream.

LEMON CUSTARD MERINGUE

For six people.

2 very large potatoes; 1 pint milk; 3 eggs; grated rind and juice of 2 lemons; 4 oz sugar; 3 tablespoons oiled butter.

Cut up the potatoes, boil in the milk and then pass through a sieve. Place the purée in a basin and beat well with a little more milk. Add the 3 yolks of eggs, grated rind and juice of the lemons, sugar and oiled butter. Mix all well together. The mixture should be like thick custard. Put into a buttered pie dish and bake in a slow oven until firm, about 1 hour. Remove from oven, whip the whites of egg stiffly, add a little sugar, whip again and pile on top of the pudding. Replace in a cool oven to set.

LEMON FOOL

For six people.

2 breakfast cups each milk and water; 3 lemons; 4 oz sugar; 2 eggs; 3 dessertspoons cornflour.

Put the water and milk into a saucepan and bring to the boil with the grated rind of 2 lemons.

Put the juice of the 3 lemons into a basin and stir in the cornflour, mix well and add to the boiling milk and water. Cook for 5 minutes. Remove from heat and cool for a few minutes. Whisk in the yolks of 2 eggs. Whip the whites to a stiff froth and fold in.

Pour into a glass dish and serve very cold.

LEMON PUDDING

For four people.

4 oz butter; 4 oz caster sugar; grated rind and juice of 1 lemon; 4 egg yolks; ¼ lb puff pastry.

Line the sides of a pie dish with thin puff pastry. Cream the butter and sugar together, add 4 yolks of eggs and the rind and juice of 1 lemon. Pour the mixture into the pie dish and cook in a moderate oven for ¾ hour.

LUNCHEON PUDDING

For four people.

6 oz finely chopped suet; 8 oz white breadcrumbs; 4 oz sugar; 4 oz raspberry jam; 2 eggs; grated rind of 2 lemons.

Put into a basin suet, breadcrumbs, sugar, raspberry jam and grated rind of lemon. Add the 2 eggs and beat all together.

Put into a greased basin and steam for 2 hours.

Serve with hot raspberry jam sauce.

MARLBOROUGH PUDDING

For six people.

6 oz butter; 6 oz sugar; 4 egg yolks; 2 egg whites; 6 oz puff pastry; apricot jam.

Line the sides of a pie dish with strips of puff pastry.

Cream butter and sugar and beat until white and fluffy, add the 4 yolks of eggs and stiffly whipped whites of 2 eggs.

Put a thick layer of apricot jam on the bottom of the pie dish, pour in the pudding mixture and bake in a moderate oven for ¾ hour.

MOUSSE DE CAFÉ WELLSBOURNE

For four people.

4 eggs; 4 oz sugar; ¾ pint cream; 4 tablespoons black coffee;
½ oz gelatine; shredded almonds.

Dissolve the gelatine in the coffee. Put into a basin over hot
water with the yolks of eggs and sugar. Beat until it thickens,
remove from heat and continue beating until cold. Whip the
whites of eggs and add alternately with the whipped cream.

Place in a glass dish and sprinkle over the shredded almonds.

NORWEGIAN CREAM

For four people.

3 eggs; 3 oz sugar; 1 pint cream; 4 tablespoons apricot jam;
2 lemons; ½ oz gelatine.

Beat the yolks of egg, sugar and grated rind of 2 lemons over
hot water until quite thick. Remove from heat and leave to
cool for about 5 minutes. Dilute the gelatine in the juice of the
lemons and add to the egg mixture, with the stiffly whipped
whites of egg.

Spread the jam on the bottom of a glass dish, add half the
cream which should be whipped, then the mixture as above,
and lastly the remainder of the whipped cream.

PAIN PERDU

For four people.

4 thick slices of stale bread, about 1 inch thick; ⅓ pint milk; 2 eggs; vanilla flavouring; ½ oz cinnamon; 4 oz sugar; butter for frying; any sort of jam.

Cut bread into 1 inch thick slices, remove crusts and cut out about 8 rounds with a medium cutter. Bring milk to the boil with half the sugar and vanilla flavouring. Allow to cool.

Pour milk into a deep dish, place in the bread rounds, allow to stand for 1½ hours, turning once. Take up and drain on a clean cloth.

Beat up the eggs in a basin, put in 2 or 3 rounds of the bread at a time, see they are well covered with egg and fry gently in hot butter. Do not allow them to touch. Sift together the remainder of the sugar and the cinnamon, and dip each fried bread into this.

Place in a circle on a hot dish and serve with any kind of hot jam in a sauce-boat.

PÊCHES THAÏS

For six people.

6 large peaches; vanilla ice cream; 1 lb fresh strawberries; 4 oz sugar.

Plunge the peaches into boiling water to remove the skins.

Poach in a thick syrup until soft. Stand aside until cold. Make a bed of vanilla ice cream and arrange the peaches around.

Serve with a purée of strawberries made by passing the fruit through a fine sieve with the sugar. Pour a little over the dish of ice and serve the remainder in a sauce-boat.

POIRES DIJON

Pears; ¾ pint fresh cream; ½ pint fresh blackcurrant purée; 4 oz sugar.

Peel, core and cut pears in half and cook in a vanilla-flavoured syrup.

Make an ice by whipping the cream until stiff, add the blackcurrant purée and sugar and freeze until hard.

Arrange the ice in a glass dish with the pears around and serve plain fresh cream separately.

POIRES À LA CONDÉ

For six people.

4 large pears; vanilla pod; 3 tablespoons rice; ¾ pint milk; sugar to taste; knobs of butter; ½ lb apricot jam; 1 tablespoon rum.

Peel, core and cut the pears in half and cook in a thin syrup with half a pod of vanilla.

Put the milk in a saucepan with the rice, bring to the boil and cook until all the milk is absorbed. Add sugar and a knob of butter. When the rice is cooked place it in a border mould, cover with a buttered paper and keep warm.

When ready to serve, turn out the rice on to a round dish and arrange the pears on the ridge of the border mould. Make the apricot jam hot, add the rum and pour over the sweet.

This dish may also be made with apples.

POIRES CRÉOLE

For four people.

4 large William pears; 1 pint milk; 3 oz sugar; 3 oz butter; vanilla pod; 2 oz fine French sago; 3 eggs; raspberry jam; whipped cream; Kirsch.

Peel and cut pears in half and cook in a thin syrup. Allow to cool and then reheat with a little Kirsch.

Put milk into a saucepan with the sugar, butter and a vanilla pod, bring to the boil and stir in the sago. Stirring all the time, boil for 10 minutes. Remove from heat and allow to cool before beating in 3 egg yolks. Fold in 3 whites of egg whipped to a stiff froth. Steam very gently in a basin or charlotte mould for ½ hour.

Turn out and arrange the hot pears around. Serve with hot raspberry sauce and whipped cream.

POMMES LIÉES

For four people.

4 large cooking apples; 6 oz sugar; vanilla essence; 1 pint milk; 3 oz seed tapioca; grated rind of 1 lemon; 3 tablespoons apricot jam.

Make a syrup with 3 parts of the sugar and a few drops of vanilla essence, and grated rind of 1 lemon. Peel and cut the apples into quarters and place in the boiling syrup. Cook until soft.

In another saucepan boil the milk, tapioca and sugar; cook until soft. Take a deep dish and pour in half the tapioca, add the cooked apples, and cover with the remainder of the tapioca. Cook in the oven for ½ hour.

Before serving make a sauce by adding some of the apple syrup to the apricot jam, and mask the top of the pudding.

POUDING MARRON

For six people.

2 lb chestnuts; 1 pint milk; vanilla flavouring; 4 oz butter; 4 oz sugar; 4 eggs; 2 tablespoons cream.

Sauce
6 small bars plain chocolate; 1 gill water; 1 oz sugar; knob of butter; tablespoon cream.

Make a cut along the skin of the chestnuts and put into a very hot oven for 5 minutes. Remove the skins and cook in vanilla flavoured milk for ½ hour. Pass the chestnuts through a sieve. Cream the butter and sugar together, add the purée of chestnuts and 4 yolks of egg. Mix well, and lastly fold in the stiffly whipped whites of egg.

Grease a basin and steam for 1½ hours.

Serve with chocolate sauce made as follows: Melt 6 bars of plain chocolate in a gill of water, add 1 oz of sugar and a knob of butter. Cook for 5 minutes and add a tablespoonful of cream before serving.

POUDING AU PAIN DE CERISE

For four people.

6 small French rolls; ½ pint milk; 4 oz cherries cut in half; 4 oz oiled butter; 4 eggs; 4 oz sugar; grated rind of 1 lemon.

Soak 6 small rolls in milk for ½ hour. Drain off as much liquid as possible. Place the soaked rolls in a basin with the sugar, oiled butter, cherries, grated lemon rind; add the egg yolks and mix well. Lastly fold in 4 stiffly whipped whites of egg.

Steam gently in a greased mould for ¾ hour.

PRINCESS PUDDING

For six people.

3 oz butter; 3 oz flour; 3 oz sugar; 4 eggs; raspberry jam.

Cream the butter and sugar together, add flour and beat for 20 minutes. Separate the eggs and add 4 yolks to the mixture. Lastly fold in 2 stiffly whipped whites of egg.

Butter 8 castle pudding moulds and put in half the mixture then 1 teaspoonful of raspberry jam and the remainder of the mixture on top.

Steam for ½ hour and serve a custard sauce separately.

POUDING ST. MARKS

For six people.

8 oz grated suet; 8 oz white breadcrumbs; 4 oz Demerara sugar; 4 eggs; 2 oz crushed ratafia biscuits; 2 oz rice flour; 2 oz plain flour; 2 tablespoons golden syrup; grated rind of 2 oranges and 2 lemons; 3 oz glacé cherries, chopped; 1 tablespoon brandy; citron peel.

Butter a mould and place 2 thin slices of citron peel at the bottom. Mix all dry ingredients together, add eggs, brandy and golden syrup. Mix well and put into the buttered mould.

Steam for 3½ hours. When cooked take out and let stand for a few minutes before turning out.

Serve with warmed cream.

POUDING SUPRÊME

For four people.

2 oz butter; 4 eggs; 2 oz flour; 2 oz caster sugar; 2 oz grated chocolate; ⅓ pint milk.

Melt the butter in a saucepan, mix in the flour, add sugar, chocolate and milk. Stir over heat until the mixture thickens, if too stiff add a little more milk. Remove from heat and cool off. Beat in 4 yolks of egg. Whip the whites until very stiff and fold into the mixture. Grease well with butter a plain charlotte mould, dust with a little flour, pour in the mixture and steam for 1 hour very carefully.

When cooked, turn out and cover with a little meringue, put back into the oven to brown.

Serve with melted chocolate to which a little cream has been added.

RAISIN PUDDING

For six people.

¾ lb beef suet cut into dice; ½ lb stoned raisins; 5 oz brown sugar; 1 Seville orange; 5 eggs; grated nutmeg; 1 oz flour.

Put the suet in a basin, add the stoned raisins, brown sugar, grated rind and juice of a Seville orange, 3 whole eggs and 2 egg yolks, nutmeg and 1 oz flour. Mix all together. Grease a pudding cloth well with butter, put in all the mixture and tie tightly with string. Put into boiling water and boil for 7 hours.

ST. GEORGE'S PUDDING

For six people.

6 oz butter; 6 oz sugar; 6 oz crushed sponge cakes; 2 oz beef suet; 1 oz rice flour; 4 oz chopped preserved fruit; 4 eggs; grated rind of 1 lemon.

Cream butter and sugar, add grated lemon rind, crushed sponge cakes, finely grated suet, rice flour and preserved fruit. Beat in the 4 yolks of egg and mix well. Lastly fold in 4 whipped whites of egg.

Steam in a greased mould for 2½ hours.

Serve with any hot jam sauce.

SOUFFLÉ DE FRAISES

For four people.

2 oz butter; 1½ oz flour; 2 oz sugar; ½ pint fresh strawberry pulp; 1 gill cream; 4 eggs.

Melt the butter in a saucepan with 1½ oz flour, add the sugar, strawberry pulp and cream. Cook for 2 minutes. Remove from heat, add 4 yolks of egg. Whip the egg whites until quite stiff and add to the mixture.

Bake in a hot oven for 10 minutes in a papered soufflé dish.

SOUFFLÉ ROTHSCHILD

For four people.

5 eggs; 3 oz sugar; 6 oz glacé fruits; wineglass of rum.

Separate the 5 eggs, add the sugar to the yolks, and 1 small glass of rum, and beat well for 5 minutes.

Cut up 6 oz glacé fruit and lay in the bottom of a soufflé case. Whip the whites of egg stiffly and add to the mixture then pour all in to the soufflé dish.

Cook in a hot oven for 10 minutes.

STONE CREAM

For four people.

1 pint cream; 4 egg yolks; ½ oz gelatine; ¼ pint milk; strawberry jam; sugar to taste.

Dissolve the gelatine in the milk and add sugar as desired.

Boil 1 pint of cream and remove from heat. Beat in the yolks of egg, add the dissolved gelatine and milk.

Cover the bottom of a fireproof dish with strawberry jam, pour in the mixture and bake in a slow oven for ½ hour. When cold glaze over with a little jelly.

SUCRE D'ÉRABLE

For four people.

4 eggs; 1 pint cream; ½ oz gelatine; 1 cup hot maple syrup.

Separate the eggs and place the yolks in a basin over hot water. Pour in the hot maple syrup and the gelatine diluted in a little of the syrup. Beat well until the mixture becomes thick. Remove from heat and allow to cool. Whip the cream until stiff and add this to the mixture. Finally add the stiffly whipped whites of egg.

WAFER PUDDING

For four people.

2 oz butter; 2 oz flour; ½ pint milk; 2 eggs.

Melt the butter in a saucepan, stir in the flour and milk and bring all to the boil, stirring all the time. Remove from heat and allow to cool for a few minutes. Separate the eggs and add the yolks, then whip the whites to a stiff froth and fold in the mixture.

Butter 6 saucers, place a little mixture on each saucer, and bake in a moderate oven for 20 minutes. Remove from saucers and fold in half.

Serve with a hot jam sauce.

SAVOURIES

BARQUETTES INDIENNE

½ lb short pastry; chutney; 2 or 3 tablespoons white sauce; 3 oz grated cheese; 2 egg yolks; seasoning.

Roll out pastry and make some boat-shaped cases; bake without browning.

Put the white sauce into a basin with the egg yolks, add grated cheese, cayenne pepper and salt. Mix well together.

Spread a little chutney in the bottom of the pastry cases, then pile in the cheese mixture.

Cook for 15 minutes in a moderate oven.

BEIGNETS WITH CHEESE

½ lb choux pastry; 4 oz grated Parmesan cheese and Gruyère cheese mixed; 1 egg yolk; cayenne pepper.

Mix the choux pastry with the grated cheese and egg yolk, add a pinch of cayenne pepper. Drop a spoonful at a time into very hot, but not boiling, deep fat. Fry slowly until a golden brown. Remove from the fat and place on kitchen paper which will absorb any surplus grease.

Serve with tomato sauce.

BEURRECK À LA TURQUE

Gruyère cheese; ½ lb nouille pastry; egg and breadcrumbs.

Cut some thick slices of Gruyere cheese into 1½ inch lengths. Roll out the nouille pastry thinly cut into oblong pieces and wrap a piece of cheese in each pastry. Egg and breadcrumb and fry in deep fat until golden brown.

BISCUITS AU FROMAGE

6 oz plain flour; 5 oz butter; 5 oz grated cheese, Parmesan and Gruyère mixed; salt and cayenne pepper; 1 egg yolk.

Rub the butter into the flour, add the grated cheese, salt and cayenne pepper. Mix into a paste with the egg yolk. Roll out and cut into desired shapes, brush over with egg, prick with a fork and bake in a moderate oven.

These can be served plain or with cream cheese piped on them when cold.

CANAPÉS AGNES

Croutes of bread; 6 oz chicken livers; 3 rashers of streaky bacon; 3 chopped shallots; 2 skinned and seeded tomatoes; 2 chopped gherkins; cayenne pepper; butter.

Fry some round croutes of bread in a little butter.

Cut up the chicken livers and bacon into small pieces and fry lightly in butter, add the chopped shallots, chopped tomatoes, chopped gherkins and a little cayenne pepper. Cook for about 10 minutes, then pile the mixture on to the croutes of bread. Serve very hot.

CANAPÉS EDOUARD VII

Slices of bread; rashers of bacon; purée of cooked mushrooms; soft herring roes; white sauce; mixed mustard; Worcester sauce.

Cut some slices of bread into fingers about 1 inch wide and fry both sides.

Place on each a slice of grilled bacon, then a little purée of cooked mushrooms, and lastly a soft herring roe which has been cooked in butter. Mix a little white sauce with some mixed mustard and a little Worcester sauce, and cover over each finger. Grill.

CANAPÉS INDIENNE

Croutes of bread; 1 tablespoon cream; 1 tablespoon milk; 2 shallots; curry powder; 3 oz cooked dried haddock; chutney; butter.

Chop the 2 shallots very finely and fry in butter, add a little curry powder, cream and milk. Cook slowly for about 10 minutes.

Fry as many croutes as needed. Melt a little butter in a saucepan and add the very finely chopped cooked haddock, heat through. Spread a little chutney on each croute, put on the haddock and then pour over the curry sauce. Place under grill to brown. Serve very hot.

CROUSTADES DE MERLUCHE

1 dried haddock; 1½ inch thick slices of bread; milk; egg and breadcrumbs; tomato sauce; grated cheese; cayenne pepper.

Cut the bread into diamond shapes, hollow out the centre, soak them in milk then egg, breadcrumb and fry each croute.

Cut the fleshy part of the haddock into small pieces, put into some tomato sauce, with grated cheese and cayenne pepper.

Make boiling hot and fill each croute with the mixture.

CROÛTES DIANE

Rashers of streaky bacon; chicken livers; mixed mustard; Worcester sauce; croutes of toast.

Roll half a chicken liver in a thin rasher of bacon which has been spread with mustard and Worcester sauce. Put several at a time on to a skewer and grill. Serve on croutes of toast.

CROÛTES À LA CONVERSE

Croutes of fried bread; purée of cooked mushroom; buttered egg; streaky bacon rashers; grated cheese; cayenne.

Cover each croute of bread with a purée of cooked mushroom. Put a little grated cheese with cayenne on a rasher of streaky bacon, roll up and grill. On each croute place a bacon roll on one side and put buttered egg on the other.

CROQUE-MONSIEUR

Sliced cooked ham; Gruyère cheese; mixed mustard; slices of toasted bread; about ¼ lb butter.

Make sandwiches by placing a thin slice of ham on some buttered toast, add a layer of thinly cut Gruyère cheese and spread on this a little mixed mustard. Place on the top another slice of buttered toast. Put under a heavy weight and press for 1½ hours. Cut these sandwiches into any shape desired and fry both sides in clarified butter.

DUCHESSE ÉCARLATTE

Choux pastry; whipped cream; finely chopped ham and chicken; cayenne pepper.

Make some small profiteroles with the choux pastry. Whip some fresh cream and stir into it some finely chopped ham and chicken and cayenne pepper. Split open the profiteroles and fill with the chicken mixture. Brush over with a little aspic jelly.

EGG PUFFS

3 eggs; 2 oz butter; 3 oz grated cheese; cream.

Put the yolks of eggs into a saucepan with the butter and 2 oz of the grated cheese and seasoning. Stir until it thickens. Remove from heat. When cool, whip the whites of eggs and fold into the mixture. Put into a greased mould and steam for 20 minutes.

Turn out on to paper, cool for a few minutes, cut into slices. Grease a fireproof dish, pour in a little cream at the bottom of the dish, place in the slices one overlapping the other, add a little more cream and grated cheese. Cook in the oven for 20 minutes.

This savoury must be served immediately it is cooked.

FONDU SUISSE

Ingredients for 1 portion.

¼ lb Gruyère cheese; ¼ bottle dry white wine; 1 small glass Kirsch; seasoning.

Cut cheese into slices and put into a dish or saucepan which can be used on the table. Place over heat, add the wine and seasoning and stir together until the cheese is melted. Add the Kirsch. Keep over heat until actual moment of eating. Have ready some bread cut into fingers with which to eat the fondu.

FRIED SARDINES

Sardines; 2 oz cheese; 1 egg; 2 oz butter; 4 oz flour; breadcrumbs; branches of parsley.

Skin and bone as many sardines as required. Make a pastry by rubbing half the quantity of butter into the flour and mixing with water. Roll out thinly.

Melt the remainder of the butter, dip in the sardines, roll them in the grated cheese then wrap the sardines singly in a portion of the pastry. Egg, breadcrumb and fry each savoury until crisp. Serve with fried parsley.

GNOCCHIS

Choux pastry; Mornay sauce; grated Parmesan cheese; cream.

Fill a forcing bag with choux pastry, take a knife and as the pastry is forced through cut off in short lengths into boiling salted water. Poach for 10 minutes.

Take up and strain and place in a buttered fireproof dish. Cover with Mornay sauce, grated cheese and cream. Brown in the oven.

MOCK CRAB

1oz butter; 6 oz cheese; 2 egg yolks; anchovy essence; a little mixed mustard; 1 dessertspoon vinegar; paprika and salt.

Melt the butter in a saucepan, add the yolks of eggs, cheese, anchovy essence, mixed mustard, vinegar, pinch of paprika and pinch of salt. Stir until the mixture becomes creamy.

Serve with fingers of hot toast.

SWISS RAREBIT

2 eggs; seasoning; 1 oz white breadcrumbs; 3 tablespoons cream; 1 oz butter; 6 oz Gruyère cheese (grated).

Beat the 2 eggs, season, add 1 oz of breadcrumbs, and cream.

Melt the butter and when hot add the cheese and stir in slowly the egg mixture. Place in a fireproof dish and put under the grill to brown.

Serve with fingers of hot toast.

TARTELETTES BEATRICE

½ lb short pastry; 3 egg yolks; chopped tongue; truffle; diced Gruyère cheese; 1 tablespoon cream; cayenne pepper.

Roll out pastry and make some small tartlet cases. Cook without browning. Put the yolks of egg into a basin and stir in the chopped tongue, truffle, diced cheese, cream and seasoning. Fill the tartlets with the mixture and bake in a slow oven.

Serve very hot.

TARTELETTES NORMANDE

½ lb short pastry; ¼ pint stiff mayonnaise; cream; cayenne pepper; 1 dozen oysters; ¼ pint shelled shrimps.

Make some small tartlets. Mix the oysters, shrimps, cream, mayonnaise and pepper together and fill the tartlets with this mixture.

Keep very cool.

TARTUSE DE JAMBON

½ lb raw lean ham; white sauce; seasoning; 1 egg yolk; butter; grated cheese; white breadcrumbs.

Pass the ham through a very fine mincer, mix with a little white sauce and seasoning, add 1 yolk of egg.

Cut some rounds of stale bread, make small sandwiches with the ham mixture. Dip into oiled butter and cover with the breadcrumbs and grated cheese mixed.

Place the savouries in a buttered pan in the oven; when slightly brown turn and brown the other side. They should be a golden colour.

PASTRY

ALMOND PASTRY

1 lb ground almonds; 1 lb caster sugar; 4 egg whites; vanilla or almond essence.

Mix all together and knead well.

CHOUX PASTRY

¼ lb butter; 4 eggs; ½ pint water; pinch of salt; 4 oz flour.

Put into a saucepan ½ pint water, ¼ lb butter and salt, and bring to the boil. When boiling mix in very quickly 4 oz flour and beat well until the mixture leaves the sides of the saucepan. Remove from the heat and allow to cool for a minute or two, then gradually add the 4 eggs one at a time.

NOUILLE PASTRY

½ lb plain flour; 2 eggs; 1 egg yolk; pinch of salt.

Put the flour into a basin, beat up the 2 eggs and 1 egg yolk and work into the flour to make a paste. If too stiff, add a little more egg.

PUFF PASTRY

1 lb plain flour; 1 lb butter; pinch of salt; squeeze of lemon juice; cold water.

Put ¾ lb flour into a basin and add the salt. Rub in about 2 oz of the butter and add sufficient water and a squeeze of lemon juice to give, when well worked together, a smooth dough. Keep aside the remaining flour for rolling out.

Roll out the pastry and place the remainder of the butter in the centre, having first squeezed out any water there may be in the butter. Fold over pastry in three and turn lengthwise.

Leave for 20 minutes in a cool place.

Roll out, fold in three and turn. Roll out fold in three and turn once more. Leave for 10 minutes. Repeat this operation twice more when the pastry will be ready for rolling to the desired thickness.

SHORT PASTRY

1 lb plain flour; 12 oz butter; pinch of salt; squeeze of lemon juice.

Rub the butter well into the flour, mix with a very small amount of water and a squeeze of lemon juice. Form into a pastry.

BISCUITS

BISCUITS MARGARET

8 oz butter; 2 oz icing sugar; 12 oz plain flour.

Rub the butter into the flour, add the sugar and knead all together. Roll out very thinly on a floured board and cut into any shapes required.

Bake in a very slow oven, taking care not to let them brown.

CHOCOLATE BISCUITS

6 oz sugar; 2 egg whites; 5 oz chocolate powder; 5 oz ground almonds; a little royal icing.

Mix together the sugar, chocolate powder and ground almonds and bind into a paste with the egg white. Roll out and cut into shapes, cover with royal icing and bake in a cool oven for about 30 minutes.

Royal icing
½ lb icing sugar; 1 egg white; ½ teaspoon lemon juice.

Sieve icing sugar. Put white of egg into a basin, gradually stir in sugar adding lemon juice, drop by drop. Beat well.

CHOCOLATE CRESCENTS

6 oz butter; 6 oz sugar; 6 oz chopped nuts; 6 oz flour; 6 oz chocolate powder; 1 egg yolk.

Rub butter into the flour, add sugar, chocolate and nuts. Bind into a paste with the egg yolk. Roll out and cut into crescent shapes. Bake in a moderate oven for about 20 minutes. When cold glaze with a glacé icing.

Glacé icing
½ lb icing sugar; 2 tablespoons warm water.

Sieve icing sugar, add water gradually until icing is of a coating consistency.

CHOCOLATE FINGERS

8 oz caster sugar; 2 oz chopped almonds; 4 oz grated chocolate; 2 egg whites; rice paper.

First slightly brown the almonds.

Warm a basin and put in the chocolate, sugar and almonds and about 1 tablespoon of water. Stir altogether then add 2 stiffly whipped whites of egg. Place the mixture in a forcing bag with a plain pipe and force on to rice paper. Cook in a very cool oven for about ½ hour.

CHOCOLATE MACAROONS

8 oz sugar; 2 egg whites; 2 oz grated chocolate; rice paper.

Mix together the sugar, egg whites and grated chocolate, beat well for at least 15 minutes. Place small heaps on rice paper and bake in a cool oven until firm to the touch, about 30 minutes.

DUCHESS BISCUITS

6 eggs; 4 oz caster sugar; 3 oz flour; vanilla essence.

Separate the eggs and whip the yolks and sugar together for 20 minutes until they are white, add vanilla essence and whip again. Fold in the flour and the stiffly whipped whites of egg. Put mixture into a forcing bag with a plain pipe and force on to a buttered and floured baking sheet. Cook in a slow oven.

HAZELNUT CRESCENTS

3½ oz caster sugar; 2½ oz butter; 3½ oz very finely ground hazelnuts; 3 oz grated chocolate; 1 oz rice flour.

Soften the butter slightly, add sugar, rice flour, finely ground hazelnuts, and grated chocolate. Make into a paste and leave for 2 hours. Roll out and cut into crescent shapes. Bake in a slow oven for about ½ hour.

HELEN'S BISCUITS

8 oz caster sugar; 4 egg whites; 3 tablespoons grated chocolate; rice paper.

Place all ingredients in a basin over boiling water and whip until very thick. Remove from heat and continue whipping until cold.

Drop small rounds on to rice paper. Bake in a very cool oven until firm to the touch.

MACAROONS

¾ lb ground almonds; ½ lb icing sugar; 2 whipped egg whites; 2 unwhipped egg whites; rice paper; blanched almonds.

Mix together the ground almonds and icing sugar, add the 2 unwhipped egg whites. Work this well together. Gradually work in the 2 whipped whites of egg. Place a spoonful of mixture on the rice paper on a baking sheet, allowing room around each macaroon for spreading. Put half a blanched almond on the centre of each macaroon. Bake in a cool oven for 20 minutes.

NUSS BUSSER

8 oz caster sugar; 8 oz chopped nuts; 4 egg whites; grated rind and juice of 1 lemon; rice paper.

Beat the whites of egg and sugar together in a basin over boiling water until the mixture becomes thick. Remove from heat and continue beating until cold. Stir in the nuts, grated rind and juice of the lemon. Drop in small rounds from a dessert spoon on the rice paper placed on a baking sheet. Dry the biscuits off in a very slow oven until firm.

NUT BISCUITS

8 oz icing sugar; 4 egg whites; 6 oz shelled splintered almonds; rice paper.

Put the icing sugar into a basin with the whites of egg. Place the basin on a saucepan of boiling water and whip the mixture until it becomes thick. Remove from heat and continue beating until the mixture is cold. Add the splintered almonds. Put spoonfuls of the biscuit mixture on to rice paper on a baking sheet, allowing a little room for spreading. Bake in a slow oven for 30 minutes, keeping them as white as possible.

SICILIAN BISCUITS

12 oz caster sugar; 4 eggs; 10 oz flour; vanilla essence; caraway seeds.

Beat the sugar and eggs in a basin over boiling water until very thick. Remove from heat and beat again until cool. Sift in the flour with a little vanilla essence. Put the mixture into a forcing bag with a plain pipe and force on to a greased baking sheet. Sprinkle over some caraway seeds and cook in a very cool oven until firm to the touch. Keep as white as possible.

VIENNA SLICES

11 oz butter; 7 oz ground almonds; 4½ oz caster sugar; 10 oz flour; vanilla essence.

Rub the butter into the flour, add sugar and ground almonds and vanilla essence. Knead into a paste.

Roll out some strips about 3 inches in width and 12 inches long. Bake in a moderate oven for 5 minutes. When cooked, sandwich with strawberry or raspberry jam, glaze with a little fondant icing. Trim the edges and cut into fingers.

CAKES

AMBROISIE

14 eggs; 1 lb caster sugar; ½ lb ground almonds; 4 oz plain flour; 4 oz potato flour; 8 oz oiled butter.

This cake keeps well and the quantities are sufficient for 2 cakes.

Separate 10 of the eggs and place the yolks in a basin with sugar. Beat for 15 minutes. Now add 4 eggs one at a time, beating well between each. Mix together the flour, potato flour and ground almonds. Stir into the beaten egg mixture, then add the oiled butter slowly. Whip stiffly the 10 whites and fold into the mixture.

Grease the cake tins with butter and dust with a little ground almonds before putting in the mixture.

Bake in a slow oven for 1 hour.

AMERICAN GINGERBREAD

½ cup margarine; ½ cup caster sugar; 2 cups plain flour; 1 cup treacle; 2 eggs; 1 teaspoon ground cloves; 1 teaspoon cinnamon; 1 teaspoon ground ginger; 1 cup boiling water; 2 level teaspoons bicarbonate of soda.

Sift all dry ingredients together except the bicarbonate of soda.

Melt the margarine and treacle together and add to the dry ingredients. Dissolve the soda in the cup of boiling water and add this to the mixture, finally adding the 2 beaten eggs.

A few sultanas may also be added.

Bake in a moderate oven for 1 hour.

BACHELOR'S BUTTONS

3 oz butter; 3 oz sugar; 1 egg; 5 oz flour; pinch of salt; vanilla essence; glacé cherries.

Rub the butter into the flour, add the sugar, work in the egg and bind all together. Pinch off pieces of the dough and roll into balls the size of a walnut. Dip them into sugar and place on a greased baking sheet, allowing a little room for each to spread. Place on each cake a small piece of glacé cherry. Bake in a medium oven for about 5 minutes or until golden brown.

BISCUIT LAYER CAKE

¼ lb butter; ¼ lb sugar; 6 oz plain flour; 1 egg; apricot jam; a little rum or cognac; few skinned and finely chopped almonds.

Rub in butter with flour, add sugar and mix with the egg. Roll out to about ⅛ inch and cut into rounds about 7 inches diameter. Bake in a slow to moderate oven until golden brown, about ½ hour. Leave at least 8 hours before using.

Mix the chopped almonds with the apricot jam and add a little rum or cognac.

Make up cake by sandwiching the biscuits and jam together. The last layer should be of biscuit and sprinkled with icing sugar.

CHOCOLATE CAKE

3 oz butter; 3 oz caster sugar; 4 oz plain flour; 2 oz grated chocolate; 2 eggs; ¼ teacup milk; ¼ teaspoon bicarbonate of soda; pinch of cream of tartar.

Cream butter and sugar together, beat in the eggs with 1 tablespoonful of the flour. Add chocolate and remainder of the flour, beat the mixture well. Dissolve the soda and cream of tartar in the milk which should be first warmed slightly. Gently add this to the cake mixture.

Bake in a moderate oven for ½ hour.

This cake can be layered and covered with glacé icing.

DELICIOUS CAKE

6 oz butter; 9 oz caster sugar; 3 eggs; 12 oz flour; coffee cupful of milk; 1 saltspoon baking powder.

Cream the butter and sugar together, add 1 tablespoon of the flour and then the eggs well beaten. Now add half the flour, beat well, add the milk and remainder of the flour sifted with the baking powder.

Bake for 1½ hours in a moderate oven.

DOBOS CAKE

Cake
5 oz sugar; 5 eggs; 4 oz flour.

Filling
10 oz slab chocolate; 10 oz caster sugar; 5 eggs; 10 oz butter; vanilla essence.

Separate the eggs and beat the 5 yolks with the 5 oz of sugar for ½ hour. Gradually fold in the flour with the 5 very stiffly beaten whites of egg.

This mixture is cooked as a layer cake, therefore it should be divided into 8 portions. Spread each portion with a palette knife to the size of a small teaplate on to a baking sheet. Bake in a medium oven until golden brown, about 20 minutes. Remove from oven and allow to cool.

Sandwich each layer with a filling made as follows:

Put a basin over hot water, place in the chocolate to melt. When melted add the sugar, eggs and vanilla essence and whip all together until the mixture is quite thick. Allow to cool slightly, then gradually mix in the butter. Beat well.

EGGLESS CHOCOLATE CAKE

5 oz self-raising flour; 1 tablespoon cocoa; 1½ oz margarine; 2 oz sugar; 1 tablespoon syrup or treacle; 1 teaspoon cinnamon; 1 teaspoon bicarbonate of soda; 2 tablespoons milk (or sufficient to make a moist consistency).

Cream sugar, margarine and warmed syrup together. Sift together flour, cocoa, cinnamon, soda and a pinch of salt. Mix well altogether and finally add the milk.

Bake in a greased tin for about ¾ hour in a fairly hot oven.

LIGHT CHOCOLATE CAKE

6½ oz butter; 6½ oz caster sugar; 6 eggs; 6½ oz grated chocolate; 6 oz plain flour; few drops vanilla essence.

Cream the butter for 15 minutes, add the yolks of eggs and sugar and beat for a further 10 minutes. Mix in the essence of vanilla, flour and grated chocolate. Fold in the stiffly whipped whites of eggs.

Put mixture into a greased and floured tin and bake for ¾ hour in a moderate oven.

Ice with glacé icing.

FRUIT CAKE

8 oz butter; 6 oz sugar; 5 eggs; 10 oz plain flour; 10 oz mixed dried fruit; 4 oz glacé cherries (cut in half); ½ teaspoon baking powder; pinch of salt.

Cream the butter and sugar together, beat in the eggs one at a time, adding a little flour to prevent curdling. Sift the remainder of the flour with the baking powder and salt and add this to the creamed mixture. Add the dried fruit and beat the mixture well.

Bake for 2 hours in a moderate oven.

GÂTEAU ADELINE

3 oz butter; 3 oz caster sugar; 2 eggs; 4 oz plain flour; 2 oz chopped glacé cherries; grated rind of a lemon and an orange; pinch of baking powder; pinch of salt.

Cream butter and sugar and beat until very white. Beat in the eggs one at a time. Stir in the chopped cherries and grated rind of orange and lemon. Add the flour sifted with the baking powder and salt. Beat well.

Bake in a moderate oven for 1 hour.

GÂTEAU HOLLANDAISE

7 oz butter; 7 oz plain flour; 2 oz brown sugar.

Rub the butter into the flour, add the sugar and rub in again. Knead until quite smooth, roll out and cut into 6 rounds the size of a small tea plate.

Place on a greased baking sheet and bake until golden brown. Sandwich the layers with marmalade.

Sift a little icing sugar on the top layer.

Note

This gâteau makes a delicious hot sweet if the layers are sandwiched with raspberry jam. It should then be served with hot raspberry sauce and whipped cream.

GÂTEAU MANQUE

8 oz butter; 1 lb caster sugar; 12 eggs; 12 oz flour.

Place 8 yolks of egg in a basin with 1 lb sugar and beat well for 15 minutes. Add 4 eggs and half the quantity of flour alternately, beating well between each addition. When very light add the remainder of the flour and the butter which must be oiled. Lastly whip the 8 remaining whites very stiffly and fold into the mixture.

Butter and flour a deep sauté pan, place in the cake mixture and bake in a moderate oven for 1 hour.

GÂTEAU VIENNOISE

8 eggs; 2 oz caster sugar; 2 oz potato flour; 2 oz ground almonds; 8 oz slab chocolate.

Separate the eggs and beat the yolks with the sugar for 15 minutes. Melt the chocolate on a dish over a saucepan of hot water. Mix together the potato flour and ground almonds and add this, with the chocolate to the egg mixture. At the last fold in the stiffly whipped whites of eggs.

Grease and lightly flour the cake tin. Bake for 1 hour in a moderate oven.

GUARDS CAKE

8 oz butter; 6 oz Demerara sugar; 16 oz flour; 6 oz sultanas; 6 oz currants; 6 oz seeded raisins (chopped); 1 oz chopped peel; ½ pint milk; 2 tablespoons vinegar; 2 teaspoons bicarbonate soda.

Rub in the butter with the flour, add all the dry ingredients. Dissolve the bicarbonate of soda in the milk, add the vinegar and mix all together. Stir well but do not beat.

Bake for 2½ hours in a medium oven.

KOUGELHOF

12 oz butter; 4 eggs and 4 egg yolks; 3 oz caster sugar; 1 lb flour; 1 oz yeast; ½ oz grated lemon rind; ½ oz cinnamon; pinch of salt; 6 almonds shelled and splintered; a little cream.

Make ready the yeast by dissolving in the cream which should be warmed slightly and a pinch of salt added.

Place the butter in a basin with the cinnamon and lemon rind and beat for 10 minutes. Add the sugar and a quarter of the flour and 2 of the eggs. Beat all well together. Work in gradually the remainder of the flour, eggs and the extra 4 yolks. When all has been mixed, continue to beat for a further 10 minutes. It will be found easier to work with the hands than with a spoon.

Smooth out the mixture in the basin making a slight well in the centre, place in the dissolved yeast and again work all this well together.

Butter a large timbale mould and sprinkle with the splintered almonds. Place in the mixture but to only half-way up the mould. Leave in a warm place until the mixture rises to the top of the mould.

Bake in a moderate oven for about ¾ hour.

LUNCH CAKE

1 lb butter; 2 lb plain flour; 1½ lb currants; 3 lb sugar; 6 eggs; grated rind of 2 lemons; grated nutmeg; 2 teaspoons baking powder; 2 tablespoons milk.

This can be baked in 1 large tin or divided in 2 smaller tins.

Cream butter and sugar together. Beat in the eggs one at a time alternately with the sifted flour and baking powder. Add the rind of the lemons, the currants and the grated nutmeg. Add the milk and beat all the mixture well before putting into the tins.

Bake for 2½ hours in a slow oven.

SEED CAKE

The weight of 3 eggs in butter and sugar; the weight of 4 eggs in plain flour; 1 tablespoonful caraway seeds; 2 oz chopped peel; 3 eggs; 1 tablespoon brandy; ½ level teaspoon baking powder.

Cream the butter and sugar together, beat in the eggs alternately with the flour. Add the caraway seeds and chopped peel and a tablespoonful of brandy. Finally, add the baking powder and then beat all well together.

Bake in a moderate oven for 1 hour.

SABLETS

8 oz butter; 8 oz caster sugar; 2 eggs; 4 oz plain flour; 4 oz potato flour; 1 oz ground almonds; grated rind of lemon; pinch of salt.

Rub the butter into the sifted flour and potato flour. Add sugar, ground almonds, grated rind of lemon, pinch of salt and work into a stiff paste with the 2 eggs.

Put on to a floured board, roll out and cut into any shapes.

Cook in a cool oven until golden brown.

SWISS ROLL

4 ½ oz caster sugar; 3 eggs; 3 oz plain flour; ½ teaspoon baking powder.

Beat the eggs and sugar together for 5 minutes. Sift in the flour and baking powder.

Grease and paper an oblong baking sheet and spread over the mixture.

Bake in a very hot oven for 8 minutes.

Turn immediately on to some sugared paper, trim edges, spread with hot jam and roll up.

WALNUT CAKE

Weight of 3 eggs in butter, in caster sugar and in plain flour; 3 eggs; pinch of salt; 1 level teaspoon baking powder; 4 oz chopped walnuts.

Cream butter and sugar together, add eggs together with 1 tablespoon flour to prevent curdling. Sift in flour, to which has been added the baking powder. Add the chopped walnuts and beat the whole mixture well.

Bake ¾ hour in a moderate oven.

WEDDING CAKE

3 lb butter; 4½ lb sugar; 36 eggs; 4 lb currants; 4 lb sultanas; 2 lb peel; 1 lb chopped almonds; 4½ lb plain flour; 1 lb glacé cherries; 1 teaspoon spice and cinnamon mixed; 1 gill brandy; grated rind of 1 orange and 1 lemon.

Cream together the butter and sugar, preferably with the hand, until very light. Beat in the eggs and sifted flour alternately. Beat all together for 10 minutes. Add gradually all the fruit, spice and grated rinds. Finally stir in the brandy.

Cover a baking sheet with salt or sand. Line the tin, or tins, with greaseproof paper, and place 3 thicknesses of brown paper on the outside of the tin.

Place cake mixture in tin, or tins, stand on the prepared baking sheet and bake in a moderate oven for the first 2 hours, lowering the heat slightly for a further 5 hours.

INDEX